P9-BAW-141

AP® COMPUTER SCIENCE PRINCIPLES CRASH COURSE®

By Jacqueline Corricelli, M.S.

Research & Education Association
Visit our website at: www.rea.com

Research & Education Association
61 Ethel Road West
Piscataway, New Jersey 08854
Email: info@rea.com

AP® COMPUTER SCIENCE PRINCIPLES CRASH COURSE®

Printed in the United States of America

Library of Congress Control Number 2017951968

ISBN-13: 978-0-7386-1234-8
ISBN-10: 0-7386-1234-0

TABLE of CONTENTS

THE EXPLORE PERFORMANCE TASK

THE CREATE PERFORMANCE TASK

PART III — THE END-OF-COURSE EXAM

PART IV — APPENDICES

PRACTICE EXAM............................*www.rea.com/studycenter*

ABOUT OUR BOOK

REA's *AP Computer Science Principles Crash Course* is designed for the last-minute studier or any student who wants a quick refresher on the AP course. The *Crash Course* is based on the AP Computer Science Principles course and exam and focuses only on the topics tested, so you can make the most of your study time.

Written by an award-winning AP Computer Science Principles test expert, our *Crash Course* gives you a concise review of the major concepts and important topics tested on the AP Computer Science Principles exam.

- **Part I** covers all the information you'll need to successfully complete your **Explore Performance Task**, including creating your computational artifact and answering the prompts to complete your task.

- **Part II** explains the intricacies of the **Create Performance Task**, including producing your video and journaling your development processes.

- **Part III** tackles the End-of-Course Exam, explaining the key topics found on the exam and strategies for successfully completing the exam.

- Handy **Appendices** cover how to convert between number systems; resources for learning programming languages; checklists for both Performance Tasks, as well as a **Glossary** of computer terms you need to know.

- **Sneak Peek**: These examples are similar to questions you might see on your AP CS Principles Exam.

- **Manage Your Time**: Estimates how much time you will need to devote to specific segments of both Performance Tasks.

ABOUT OUR ONLINE PRACTICE EXAM

How ready are you for the AP Computer Science Principles exam? Find out by taking **REA's online practice exam** available at *www.rea.com/studycenter*. This test features automatic scoring, detailed explanations of all answers, and diagnostic score reporting that will help you identify your strengths and weaknesses so you'll be ready on exam day.

Whether you use this book throughout the school year or as a refresher in the final weeks before the exam, REA's *Crash Course* will show you how to study efficiently and strategically, so you can boost your score.

ABOUT REA

Founded in 1959, Research & Education Association (REA) is dedicated to publishing the finest and most effective educational materials—including study guides and test preps—for students of all ages.

Today, REA's wide-ranging catalog is a leading resource for students, teachers, and other professionals. Visit *www.rea.com* to see a complete listing of all our titles.

ACKNOWLEDGMENTS

We would like to thank Pam Weston, Publisher, for setting the quality standards for production integrity and managing the publication to completion; John Cording, Vice President, Technology, for coordinating the design and development of the REA Study Center; Larry B. Kling, Vice President, Editorial, for his overall direction; Diane Goldschmidt, Managing Editor, and Alice Leonard, Senior Editor, for editorial project management; Kathy Caratozzolo for typesetting; Karen Lamoreux for copyediting; Ellen Gong for proofreading, and Jennifer Calhoun, for file preparation.

In addition, we extend our special thanks to Robert Juranitch, M.S.Ed., for his technical review of the manuscript. Mr. Juranitch currently teaches AP Computer Science Principles at The University School of Milwaukee, Milwaukee, Wisconsin.

ABOUT OUR AUTHOR

Jacqueline Corricelli teaches AP Computer Science Principles at Conard High School, West Hartford, Connecticut. A public school educator for more than 14 years, Ms. Corricelli designed curriculum to allow her school to be among the first to offer AP Computer Science Principles, and has served as a College Board pilot instructor for the course.

In 2017, Ms. Corricelli was one of just 10 teachers to be honored with the Computer Science Teaching Excellence Award. The international award is sponsored by Infosys Foundation USA; the Association for Computing Machinery, the world's leading computing society; and the Computer Science Teachers Association.

Ms. Corricelli is also a recipient of the Presidential Award for Excellence in Mathematics and Science Teaching, the highest honor bestowed by the United States government for K–12 mathematics and science (including computer science) teaching.

The author, a former radar systems engineer, is a member of the Connecticut State Department of Education CS Advisory Group, created to improve access to and define computer science education at the state level.

Ms. Corricelli earned her B.A. in mathematics and statistics from the University of Connecticut and her M.S. in mathematics secondary education at Westfield State University in Massachusetts.

Dedicated to my daughter Genevieve, who inspires me every day.

Keys for Success
on the AP Computer
Science Principles Exam

The AP Computer Science Principles course and exam can be completed successfully by anyone who has access to a computer and a love of learning. In your research about this AP course and exam, you have probably realized that there are quite a few different ways to learn what you need to know. You may have even followed the "rabbit holes" of information online and learned that you need a way to (1) get the essential knowledge, (2) figure out what you need to do to score well, and (3) find one resource (rather than twenty different tabs) that you can trust.

This *Crash Course* is designed to help you get the best score on your AP Computer Science Principles exam by providing the information that you need to know, helping you manage your time to complete the performance tasks, and helping you find resources that you can trust.

Remember: Succeeding on the AP Computer Science Principles exam is definitely within your reach, especially when you study strategically with this *Crash Course* book!

KEY 1: UNDERSTAND THE STRUCTURE OF THE EXAM

The AP Computer Science Principles exam consists of three parts: two performance tasks and an End-of-Course multiple-choice exam. 40% of your score comes from the two performance tasks and 60% of your score comes from the End-of-Course Exam. The two performance tasks are completed and submitted to the College Board prior to taking the End-of-Course Exam, which is administered in May.

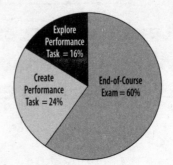

- **The Explore Performance Task**

  The actual title of this task is "Explore—Impact of Computing Innovations." This task is worth 16% of your AP exam score and takes about 8 hours to complete. In this task you will research a computing innovation that interests you.

  To complete the task, you will submit a computational artifact and written responses to prompts provided by the College Board. Part I of this book is devoted to helping you prepare for and execute the Explore Performance Task.

- **The Create Performance Task**

  Also known as the "Create—Applications from Ideas" task, this task is worth 24% of your AP exam score and takes about 12 hours to complete. This task involves creating a program as a way to express yourself, solve a problem, or understand something better.

  In this task you will design a program of your choice and submit a video of your program running and your program code. You will also submit written responses about your program and your development process to prompts provided by the College Board. Part II of this book focuses on helping you with the Create Performance Task.

  Both performance tasks will require that you have access to a computer to type your responses and find solutions to research questions and programming problems.

- ## The End-of-Course Exam

  The final part of the AP Computer Science Principles course is the End-of-Course Exam. This is a multiple-choice exam that contains approximately 74 questions with four answer choices: (A) through (D). It is worth 60% of your AP exam score, and 2 hours is allotted to complete the exam.

> *The two Performance Tasks are written, researched, designed, and created by you. These are worth 40% of your exam and you will know the prompts, rubric, and how to maximize your score by careful planning and from tips in this book.*

KEY 2: UNDERSTAND HOW THE EXAM IS SCORED AND WHAT IT MEANS

Your Explore Performance Task, your Create Performance Task and your End-of-Course Exam will all be scored independently.

The End-of-Course Exam is scored by machine. There are two types of questions and there is no partial credit for either question type.

(1) Single-Select Multiple Choice—only one answer choice is correct

(2) Multiple-Select Multiple Choice—two answer choices are correct

Each of the 74 questions is worth one point and your score is based on the number of questions answered correctly. Points are not deducted for incorrect answers, and no points are awarded for unanswered questions. For the multiple-select multiple-choice questions, you must choose *both* of the correct answers to receive credit.

The Explore Performance Task and Create Performance Task are scored during the annual AP Exam Reading, which takes place in June. AP Computer Science Principles teachers and college instructors apply a scoring guide for these items and award points based on those guidelines.

The scores from your performance tasks and the end-of-course exam are then combined and converted to a 1-to-5 AP scale.

The College Board uses a formula (which changes slightly from year to year) to rank your combined performance task grades and your End-of-Course exam grade into five categories:

5 = Extremely Well Qualified

4 = Well Qualified

3 = Qualified

2 = Possibly Qualified

1 = No Recommendation

Some colleges and universities accept scores of 3, 4, or 5 for college credit, but some only accept 4s and 5s. Some colleges do not award credit for an AP test, so it is important that you research the policies of the colleges you are interested in attending. Also, be aware that colleges and universities can change their AP acceptance policies at any time. Stay up-to-date by checking the latest AP policies on their websites.

Test Tip

Even if a college does not award placement credit for an AP exam, taking an AP test may strengthen your college application because you rose to the "AP challenge."

KEY 3: UNDERSTAND THE CONTENT TESTED ON THE END-OF-COURSE EXAM.

The topics that make up the End-of-Course Exam are as follows:

Topic	Percentage of Questions on End-of-Course Exam
Algorithms	20%
Programming	20%
Abstraction	19%
Data & Information	18%
The Internet	13%
Global Impact	10%

Part III of this book focuses on helping you get ready for these questions and includes sample multiple-choice questions.

KEY 4: UNDERSTAND THE COLLEGE BOARD'S DIGITAL PORTFOLIO

Using the College Board's Digital Portfolio, a Web-based application, you will submit five final performance task artifacts, three artifacts for the Create task and two artifacts for the Explore task.

Your AP Teacher will receive approval at the start of the school year to access the Digital Portfolio. He or she will set up a class that you will need to access. If you have taken an SAT or PSAT, you most likely already have an account with the College Board. You will use the same information to go to *www.collegeboard.org/ digital-portfolio* to connect your account to your AP Computer Science Principles class. Your AP teacher will confirm your enrollment.

Once done, you'll be all set to submit your artifacts, your written responses for the performance tasks, and indicate your intent to take the End-of-Course Exam.

Remember, your final performance task artifacts and written responses must be submitted by the end of April.

KEY 5: SUPPLEMENT YOUR *CRASH COURSE*

REA's *Crash Course* contains *essential* information for the AP Computer Science Principles tasks and End-of-Course Exam. You should, however, supplement this book with materials from your course and the College Board.

The AP Computer Science Principles Course Description booklet from the College Board shares information about the course and the exam, and includes sample questions. Additionally, the College Board's AP Central website (*www.apcentral.collegeboard. org*) contains review materials, including sample responses for the performance tasks and scoring guidelines.

KEY 6: HANDLING EXAM DAY

1. Plan to show up at the exam site at least 20 minutes before the scheduled start time for the exam.

2. Bring two fresh No. 2 pencils with clean erasers and two working blue- or black-ink pens.

3. Be prepared to turn in your cell phone and other electronic devices at the beginning of the exam. You might want to just leave them home!

4. The exam proctor will read a lot of instructions—be patient. Plan to spend more than the allotted 2 hours at the exam site.

5. Answer every multiple-choice question, even if you have to guess. Remember, there is no deduction for an incorrect answer but no points can be earned for unanswered questions. If you're stuck, give it your best guess.

6. When you're done, relax . . . sit back and wait for your passing score to arrive!

Test Tip

Use the Test Tips scattered throughout this Crash Course to help you save time as you prepare for your tasks and exam.

PART I
THE EXPLORE PERFORMANCE TASK

Introduction to the Explore Performance Task

 OVERVIEW

A. The Explore Performance Task consists of three main parts:

1. Researching a computing innovation.

2. Creating a computational artifact.

3. Writing responses to prompts in the task, including in-text citations.

B. The task is worth 16 percent of your AP Computer Science Principles score.

C. In the Explore Performance Task, you will do research to create a computational artifact. This artifact is visual, graphical, or video content created using a computer. The research you will be doing to complete this task has to do with a computing innovation.

D. The Explore Performance Task should take a minimum of 8 hours to complete. For example, if you spend 45 minutes each day on this task, it will take you a minimum of 11 days to finish it.

E. This task, along with the Create Performance Task (see chapters 8–15), needs to be completed and submitted to the College Board using the Digital Portfolio by April 30.

II. ABOUT THE EXPLORE PERFORMANCE TASK

A. The Explore Performance Task is a focused research project about a computing innovation.

B. The Explore Performance Task must be done independently by you. No collaboration with others is permitted.

C. Be sure to read about the Explore Performance Task, as well as the scoring guidelines, available online at *apcentral. collegeboard.org.*

D. To maximize your score, answer each prompt and always cite any source you are using.

III. MAXIMIZE YOUR SCORE—BRAINSTORM AND RESEARCH

A. Brainstorm

1. Your topic is the center of your Explore Performance Task. The topic should be a computing innovation that satisfies *all* of the following requirements:

   i. The innovation must be a computing innovation. To determine if it is a computing innovation, ask yourself the following question: Does a computer or program/ code make it work? If your answer is "no," it is not a computing innovation, and you should not use this innovation for this project. If your answer is "yes," this innovation may be a good fit for this project.

Test Tip

If you're having trouble finding good sources while doing your research, think about changing topics. Changing your topic will get harder later on when you are more invested with a particular computing innovation.

ii. The computing innovation will have, did have, or already has had the potential to have both beneficial and harmful significant effects on a society, a culture, or an economy.

iii. The computing innovation consumes, produces, and transforms data.

iv. The computing innovation raises at least one data storage concern, data privacy concern, or data security concern.

For you to get the most credit for this task, the innovation you choose must be a computing innovation. Search until you find a computing innovation that you want to research and write about.

2. In the Explore Performance Task, you will also create an artifact that should educate a viewer about the innovation you have chosen. Your artifact should be largely non-text, such as an illustration, video, or audio that explains the computing innovation's intended purpose, function, or effect.

3. Your artifact must accomplish all of the following:

    i. clearly identify the innovation by name;

    ii. provide an illustration, representation, or explanation of the innovation's purpose, function, or effect;

    iii. show that you understand that the computer is a tool to express your innovation's purpose, function, or effect in a way that you could not do by words alone;

    iv. be a video, audio, or pdf file created by you using a computer.

Be sure you understand the difference between a feature of your innovation, and your innovation's purpose, function, or effect. For example, if a self-driving car is your computing innovation, a feature would be the sensors that allow the computer in the car to process information better at night than human eyes. The effect would be that the car is safer and accidents are prevented at nighttime. Effect is an impact on others due to the innovation. Purpose is the reason the innovation was created—for example, how it helps others who may not own the innovation. Function is how the innovation works. In your artifact and your research, be sure to cover not just your innovation's inner workings, but also how it works and impacts our world.

4. When brainstorming your topic, choose a topic that is meaningful to you.

5. Your written responses and your artifact are based on your research of the computing innovation.

6. When generating ideas, ask yourself the following questions:

   i. What computing innovation has made a difference in my life?

   ii. What computing innovation inspired me to want to learn more about computer science?

   iii. What computing innovation is related to my future "dream job"?

   iv. What computing innovation do I use in my spare time?

Allow 2 to 3 hours to research your topic for the Explore Performance task.

B. Research

1. In this step, you will decide on your topic and research it.

2. Later in this performance task when you write responses to the prompts (see chapters 4–7), you will need to cite at least three online or print sources.

    i.   Two of the sources must have been created after the end of the last academic year.

    ii.   At least two of the sources must be available online or in print; your third source may be online, in print, or a personal interview with an expert on the computing innovation.

3. You will use the Internet for much of your research. Be sure you are using credible sources.

4. Keep in mind the following criteria when evaluating whether a source is credible or not:

    i.   Purpose—The article should be written to inform, not persuade or sell.

    ii.   Author—The author(s) should be named and related to the field that you are researching.

    iii.   Date—The date of the source should be current for your innovation. Remember, at least two sources need to have been created after the end of the last academic year.

5. Here is a partial list of reputable sources to help begin your research:

    i.   ACM TechNews (*technews.acm.org*)—This collection of computer science innovations is usually current, and the edition date is found on the homepage. The archives also contain resources that may be timely enough to use for your task.

    ii.   Science Daily (*sciencedaily.com*)—This is a constantly evolving collection of articles on scientific innovations. Most articles are current. Many of the discoveries noted are a direct result of computing innovations.

    iii.   National Public Radio (NPR) Technology News (*npr.org/sections/technology*)—This is a collection of technology articles and/or recordings related to current issues.

    iv.   Google Scholar (*scholar.google.com*)—This Google search tool returns scholarly articles on topics. It may be best to use this tool after you have narrowed down your choices on the innovation you want to write about for your task.

v. Futurism (*futurism.com*)—This is a website with links to cutting-edge science articles, infographics, and stories.

To give you an idea of what you are working toward, now is a great time to check out the Explore Performance Task samples in the "Sample Responses to Performance Tasks" area on AP Central (apcentral.collegeboard.org). The College Board has collected samples of work completed by students just like you. Scores and feedback are provided to help you understand how the task and scoring guidelines are used together to determine your grade.

6. Make sure you have researched the *impact* of your topic.

   i. When doing your research, be on the lookout for both the harm and the benefit of the innovation to a society, a culture, or an economy.

   ii. Look for at least three good sources when you begin. If you need more sources, you can find them while you are writing.

   iii. One of the effects (harmful or beneficial) needs to be significant. To maximize your score for this performance task, you need a statement that shows broad social, economic, or cultural impact. The impact needs to affect more people than just those who own or use the innovation.

   iv. **Cultural Impact:** To show *cultural impact,* you will need to show evidence that the innovation has caused rules of behavior to change among people in society. Below is an example of how you might give evidence of cultural impact.

   ▸ Example of an innovation with cultural impact: social media

▸ Evidence: You might cite the following research:

  – Source 1: An article stating that elections have been impacted by social media "get-out-the-vote" campaigns that result in higher voter turnout.

  – Source 2: A research paper called "Social Media's Impact on Culture," written by an expert in sociology, explains how many different aspects of culture have been impacted by social media. The impacts are connected to the innovation, and it is clear how the impacts to culture are caused by the innovation.

  – Source 3: Interview with a person who had his cancer treatment paid for by strangers due to a social media campaign. This shows how the person was able to use the innovation to pay for his treatment. In addition, the interviewee talks about a "culture of hope" that has grown for people suffering from cancer who are empowered by using social media as a way to fund their treatment.

▸ Why these sources work: These three sources show that social media is impacting many parts of our culture, and this innovation is cited as the cause of these impacts.

The key to writing a good research paper is to find evidence of every effect you claim. The cause is what you find; the effect is the argument you make in the research paper. The argument that connects the cause to the effect is yours. You are writing the argument, but your proof is from other sources.

v. **Social Impact:** To show *social impact,* you will need to show that the innovation impacted a society in some way. Below is an example of how you might show evidence of social impact.

- ▸ Example of innovation with social impact: graphing calculators

- ▸ Evidence: Looking at the math classroom as the society, the following research is cited:

    - Source 1: The website for the company that makes the calculator provides many lessons for teachers to use in the classroom. The teachers on the website post comments that indicate how the lessons have helped students learn. Several talk about the time and paper saved by not having to plot by hand.

    - Source 2: Your classroom has used some of these lessons, and your teacher created a test question that required use of the calculator.

    - Source 3: You interviewed your friend about the graphing calculator and she talks about how much easier graphing can be with the calculator. She talks about how she and her friends enjoy working through math problems.

- ▸ Why these sources work: First, the society is defined (the math classroom). Then, the three sources each focus on different aspects of the society. There is evidence that the innovation influenced the teacher, the test (class as a whole), and the student who was interviewed.

vi. **Economic Impact:** To show *economic impact,* you need to show the financial influence of the innovation. Below is an example of how you might show evidence of economic impact.

- ▸ Example of innovation with economic impact: YouTube

- ▸ Evidence: The following research is cited:

    - Source 1: News story about a musician who began her career using this innovation. She made enough money via YouTube so she can now focus on music full-time.

- Source 2: Step-by-step instructions exist to help anyone get started making money on YouTube.

- Source 3: You found this document online: "Recording Studios Cannot Keep Doors Open." The document states that traditional recording studios are making less money and cites YouTube as a factor in the decline of traditional recording studios.

▸ Why these sources work: Each source included information about the financial influence of the innovation. The influence affects the individual, the community, and the business world.

The impact you will write about needs to be directly caused by your innovation. If you choose an impact that could be caused by many computing innovations (such as hacking), the impact will not be specific enough.

C. Finishing and Organizing Your Research

1. Whatever computing innovation you choose to write about, you need to be able to explain it in terms of *impact*. Looking for the impact early (and often) will help you decide the story you want to tell about your computing innovation.

2. At least one of your statements about impact will need to show the broad impact to society, economy, or culture.

   i.   This statement could be about a harmful or a beneficial effect.

   ii. The effect needs to be beyond those that own or use the innovation.

   iii. The effect to society, economy, or culture is *caused* by the innovation even if people do not own or use it.

3. Evidence will show up in surprising places. All of the following can be used as evidence:

   i. Interviews (online, radio, conversations with experts)

   ii. Articles

   iii. A survey that you created

   iv. An online blog that is monitored by an expert in the field

   v. A YouTube video created by an expert in the field

4. Use the following chart to help you keep your thoughts organized.

What is the computing innovation?	
What is the harm of this innovation? (What is the impact to society, culture, or the economy directly caused by this innovation?)	
What is a benefit of this innovation? (What is a gain to society, culture, or the economy directly caused by this innovation?)	

5. Be aware of the scope of your topic.

   i. Your topic is too narrow if you are having difficulty finding resources on your innovation. To fix this, try the following:

   ▸ Can you describe the topic more generally?

   ▸ Instead of searching for a particular microchip or manufacturer, search for the innovation type. For example, instead of searching "Microchip in Lenovo ThinkPad," use "Microchip Technology."

ii.   Your topic is too broad if you are getting too many results from your search. To fix this, try the following:

▸ Limit your search term.

  − Use fewer words.

  − Use the keyword "and" to find sources that have more than one thing of value to you in your research.

▸ Instead of searching for "The Internet," search for a particular aspect of the Internet, such as "search engines on the Internet."

6. Do a final check of your innovation's impact.

i.   You will be done with your initial research for this project when you have a meaningful innovation that meets *all* of the following requirements:

☐ Yes, the innovation means something to me.

☐ I found evidence of harm to society, culture, or the economy directly caused by the innovation.

☐ I found evidence of a benefit to society, culture, or the economy directly caused by the innovation.

☐ At least one of these impacts (harmful or beneficial) affects those who do not own or use the innovation.

☐ I am in the process of finding several (at least three) reputable sources.

7. Store and organize your sources.

i.   Keep your sources in a numbered list. It is easiest to cite them right away while you have the sources and information fresh in your mind.

ii.   Use a standard citation format. There are several online tools you can use to create the format. Typical examples of formats are: MLA (Modern Language Association), APA (American Psychological Association), or Chicago (Chicago Manual of Style). Search "Citation Tool" in any online search engine to find resources to help you create these citations.

    iii. Online citations need to show: permanent URL, author, title, source, date you retrieved the source, and, if possible, the date the reference was written or posted.

    iv. Print sources need to cite: the author, title (of magazine, article, or book), page number(s), publisher, and the date of publication.

    v. Interview sources need to cite: the name of the person interviewed, the date that the interview occurred, and the person's position in the field you are researching.

    vi. After you cite your source, write a note about why you kept the source. You will remove these notes before your final submission, but this will make it easier to cite the source later in the written portion of this task. On the note record:

        ▸ What is the innovation?

        ▸ Is the source about a harm or a benefit?

        ▸ Does this source show broad impact, even to those who do not use or own the innovation?

8. Research the *data* associated with your topic.

    i. The computing innovation you choose for your Explore Performance Task needs to be explained in terms of the data the innovation uses.

    ii. Data types include: integers, numbers, Booleans, text, image, video, audio, or signals. Whatever innovation you choose, be sure you understand how data is reduced to these data types so you can write about it in your written response.

    iii. To be sure you have researched your data fully, you should:

        ▸ Find data that is important for your innovation.

          – Start with a search, such as "How does (your innovation) work?" or "Data inside (your innovation)."

- Keep this research broad. The data you are describing is general. Do not use jargon or acronyms. You do not need to know about programming to answer this question.

- The data you find should be specific. When you read the data description, you should be able to tell how the computer stored it.

▸ Describe how the innovation uses the data.

- Explain how the data is received, changed, *or* output by your innovation. (Note that you only need to show *one* of these!)

▸ Identify one data concern in terms of a storage, privacy, or security concern directly related to the innovation.

Note that the data you identify as important to your innovation will be used two more times in your Explore Performance Task, so make sure you have researched it well. You will need to identify the data used by the innovation, explain how this data moves through the innovation (how the data is input, output, or transformed), and also identify where the data is vulnerable.

iv. Look over your existing resources. You might find information about data in some of these.

v. If you are having trouble identifying data because your innovation is very specific or very new, try these options:

▸ Option 1: Widen the scope of your research. Ask yourself the following questions:

- What data do users of this innovation need to input to make the innovation work? This data could be a sound file, an image file, or characters. Be open-minded about what data might look like.

> – What stops the innovation from working? This will help you to see the data since a lack of data might make the innovation stop working.

▸ Option 2: Change your approach to your research.

> – Focus on vulnerabilities. You might find legal cases related to data being illegally recorded, or experts guessing where a system might be vulnerable.

> – Find a parallel innovation. Find an innovation that is similar to yours, but that has more resources. This requires two parts to make a valid argument:

> a. Be sure that you can draw enough parallels to make a case about how the same issues would show up for your innovation.

> b. Then look for the data issues that came up for that parallel innovation.

9. Make a final check of your data.

   You will know you are finished with this step when you have a computing innovation that meets all of the following requirements:

   ☐ I have examples of data used by my innovation.

   ☐ I have researched data enough that I have found sources that explain how data is decomposed to a fundamental type by the innovation.

   ☐ I have examples that explain how the innovation consumes, produces, and/or transforms data.

   ☐ I have a few resources that identify at least one data storage, privacy, or security concern related to the innovation.

   ☐ The resources I have are reputable.

Creating the Explore Performance Task Computational Artifact

I. **CONTENTS OF THE ARTIFACT**

A. A successful artifact must do *all* of the following:

1. It must clearly identify the computing innovation.

2. It must have been created by a human using a computer, and can be (but is not limited to) any of the following:

   i. a program

   ii. an image

   iii. an audio

   iv. a video

   v. a presentation

   vi. a webpage file

3. It must provide an illustration, representation, or explanation of the computing innovation's purpose, function, or effect.

4. It must convey the purpose, function, or effect of the innovation in a way that could not be done using just words.

Allow 2 to 3 hours to plan and brainstorm your artifact for the Explore Performance Task.

II. PLANNING AND BRAINSTORMING THE ARTIFACT

A. Plan the artifact.

1. Decide on the type of statement you want to make with your artifact.

   i. Do you want to make a creative statement?

   ii. Do you want to inform your audience?

   iii. The artifact could be (but is not limited to) an infographic, an advertisement, an infomercial, a "menu," a graph or data display, an animation, a short movie, or a tutorial.

2. Know the requirements of the artifact. The artifact must be:

   i. a video or an audio file (less than 1 minute and under 30 MB), or a PDF (less than three pages).

   ii. created with computing tools to illustrate, represent, or explain your innovation's intended purpose, function, or effect.

   iii. created using acceptable formats for multimedia file types which include: *.mp3, .mp4, .wmv, .avi, .mov, .wav, .aif,* or *.pdf.*

3. Brainstorm the artifact.

   i. Write down what you know about the computing innovation you researched in the last step. Include:

      ▸ two positive impacts and two negative impacts of your innovation.

      ▸ something you learned about how the data is used, input, or transformed.

      ▸ the purpose of the innovation: Why was it created? What problem does it solve?

      ▸ information about how the innovation works.

ii. Think of images.

▸ Think of how you can convey meaning by using images.

▸ Write down three ideas, no matter how ridiculous or impossible they may seem.

▸ Sketch your ideas. As you do, consider the following questions:

  – Can you put the ideas into one image?

  – Can you think of a way to show the purpose, function, or effect of the innovation in one computational artifact?

  – What understandings do you have about your innovation that might not be easy for others to know by just looking at the innovation?

  – How can you explain these understandings with images or a story?

III. INITIAL SETUP

A. At a minimum, you will need:

1. word processing software; and

2. regular Internet access, or a flash drive and occasional Internet access (at a library or coffee shop, for example).

B. To start, do the following:

1. Keep a journal. The written part of the Explore Performance Task requires that you explain the steps you took to create your artifact. To jog your memory, keep a journal with entries that record:

   i. the date(s)

   ii. the tool(s) you used

   iii. an explanation as to what this tool will help to illustrate, represent, or explain regarding the purpose, function, and effect of the innovation (or: How did this tool do this?)

2. Find out who your point of contact is for submitting your performance tasks.

   i. Approach a teacher authorized to create a class and to approve your tasks on the College Board's Digital Portfolio website. Whoever is authorized for this position will be in charge of handing your performance task in to the College Board by the late April deadline.

   ii. Keep communication open and clear to be sure this teacher knows your intent to submit your performance tasks and take your End-of-Course Exam in May.

   iii. You cannot access the Digital Portfolio without an authorized teacher's assistance, so communicate with your teacher as soon as possible.

3. With your teacher's assistance, access the College Board's Digital Portfolio at *digitalportfolio.collegeboard.org*. You will

need to log in once you access the website. Note that you may already have an account set up with the College Board. SAT test takers often set up an account to get their scores. You can log in using that same information.

i. Read the directions for the use of the Digital Portfolio.

ii. Download the Explore Performance Task template. This is the tool you will use to submit your written responses.

IV. COMMONLY USED TOOLS

A. Your computational artifact will be a video, audio, or PDF file. The following multimedia file types are accepted: *mp3, mp4, wmv, avi, mov, wav, aif,* or *pdf.* The PDF must not exceed three pages, and the video or audio files must not exceed 1 minute in length or 30 MB in size.

B. To support these requirements, you will likely need tools such as:

1. **Image creation tool.** This is a tool that allows you to process images from any source. It is probably called a "snip" or "snipping tool." Search for one on your computer. If you are using an online image, be sure to cite the source.

2. **PDF creation tool.** This tool allows you to create PDFs. PDF stands for "Portable Digital Format." If you like using Google Docs, you can download files as PDFs by choosing the File dropdown menu, then selecting "Download As" a PDF. In most other environments, you can choose PDF as a print option.

3. **Screen recording tool.** This is a tool to record your screen movements. This is especially helpful if your artifact involves a website, blog, or data display that requires viewing multiple screens. ScreenCast-O-Matic (*screencast-o-matic.com*) works well for this. You will need to download a small file, but it will work in both Windows and Mac environments. If you are using the Linux operating system, SimpleScreenRecorder is a good choice.

USING TOOLS THAT ARE ALREADY ON YOUR COMPUTER

A. If you do not have an Internet connection, you can create your computational artifact using tools that you already have on your computer.

    1. Reasons you may prefer using the data and tools on your computer include:

        i.   You have a favorite tool (photo editor, music editor, etc.) on your computer.

        ii. In the written portion of this task, you will need to explain your process. Having the tool on your computer may make this easier.

B. The process you use to create your artifact will depend on your unique set of skills, the time you have to learn new skills, and the type of innovation you chose. Start by determining what you can already do on your computer.

C. The following tools may already be on your computer and may be helpful for completing your Explore Performance Task:

    1. **Photo editor.** A photo editor lets you edit an image file. A file is an image if it has a *.jpg* or *.png* extension in the filename. If you don't have a photo editor on your computer, you can download a photo editor program for free. Pixlr Editor is free, and it works for Windows or Mac users. You can download it as an app at *pixlr.com*. For Linux users, Pixeluvo is a good choice of photo editor.

    2. **Presentation creator.** This tool is used oftentimes to organize your thoughts as a sequence of images and/or words. In situations such as a timeline or photo collage, presentation software may help you organize your thoughts. You could create the presentation and submit it as a sequence of images or you could narrate it with a video maker. Two common examples of presentation software are PowerPoint for Microsoft or Keynote for Mac.

    3. **Video maker or video editor.** This tool is used to make and edit videos. A file is a video file if it ends with one of

the following extensions: *.avi, .mov, .qt, .wmv,* or *.mp4.* If you double-click on a video, an option to edit may already accompany the video. A video editor is often included with the operating system of a computer. For example iMovie is downloadable from the Mac App Store for Mac computers. Windows Movie Maker is included with PCs. Cinelerra is a popular downloadable video editor for Linux users.

4. **Sound editor.** With this tool, you can edit sound files. Typical extensions for a sound file include: *.mp3, .wav,* or *.aif.* If you double-click on a sound file, there may already be an option to edit that file. Many sound editors are included with the computer's operating system. For example, WavePad may be included with your operating system. You can also download it at the Mac App Store or from the website *nch.com.au.* A downloadable editor called Audacity works for the Linux/Gnu operating system, as well as Windows or Mac. You can download it from the website *audacityteam.org.*

5. **Spreadsheet software.** Spreadsheets allow you to organize sets of data into columns and rows. Probably the most common spreadsheet program is Excel, which is available for both Windows and Mac operating systems. Apple has a Mac-specific spreadsheet program called Numbers. This software is very helpful if you want to turn a set of data into an image, such as a graph.

D. Understand the tools available on your computer.

1. Familiarize yourself with the tools you already have.

2. While you are working, journal about how these tools worked and what you liked (or did not like) about them.

3. Think about the story you could tell about your innovation with each of these tools. Typical stories told by successful artifacts include:

   i. The artifact informs the viewer about how the innovation works.

   ii. The artifact shows the impact of the innovation.

E. Right now, you have the tools you need if:

1. you have an idea about how to use these tools to tell a story about your innovation.

2. you can explain why you chose these tools to tell your story.

Keep in mind that creating this artifact is an ongoing process. You may change your mind and decide you need more tools later.

VI. USING ONLINE TOOLS

A. If you are using a computer with limited storage, or if you are not familiar with the tools on your computer, you might find an Internet search helpful. Here are several suggestions:

1. There are many free tools available online. Some can be used in a browser, while others require a download. Exercise care when downloading tools, and make sure they are compatible with your computer system.

2. Search for what you want to do and you will likely find several examples of photo editors, video makers/editors, sound editors, and spreadsheets. Keep in mind the following precautions:

   i. When you use a search engine, you are vulnerable. Do not download software that you do not trust. Be careful about which websites you download your images from. Be sure the images you use are public domain or that you have permission to use them, and be sure to credit other people's images that you use.

   ii. Some tools will require that you pay to download and use them. You may not find that out until the final step. Understand their policies before you decide to use their tool.

3. Avoid plagiarism by citing sources of images.

   i. Jot down where you found the image (link, author, site), or complete the citation (MLA, APA, etc.) as you find each image.

   ii. Use sites first that offer Commons and other public domain images. These sites offer collections created by people who want to share their work. Search "Commons Site and Sounds," for example, to find a site with sound files that are available for use. An example of a commons site is Wikimedia Commons (*commons.wikimedia.org*).

4. Remember, your goal for your artifact is to create a story about the function, purpose, or effect of your innovation. The most successful artifacts use a computer to do something that you cannot do with words.

Test Tip

Be sure you choose tools to work with for specific reasons related to your innovation. Remember, you will need to explain why you chose your tools in the written portion of this task. Your explanation will need to show that you weighed the pros and cons of those particular tools in your final decision.

5. Experiment with this partial list of tools. Determine if they can be of help to you:

   ▸ Animoto (*animoto.com*)—Turn still images into a video, add text and modify.

   ▸ Audacity (*audacityteam.org*)—Edit sound files; requires a download.

   ▸ Canva (*canva.com*)—Create flyers and beautiful combinations of images.

   ▸ Desmos (*desmos.com*)—Graph plotter and tools for investigation.

   ▸ Futurism (*futurism.com*)—Interesting collection of links to research and developments.

> ▸ Google Books NGram Viewer (*books.google.com*)—Search books through the centuries for word and/or name appearances.

> ▸ Infogram (*infogram.com*)—Create informative graphic collages.

> ▸ Interactivate (*shodor.org/interactivate*)—Tools to create using math and science.

> ▸ MindMeister (*mindmeister.com*)—Create flowcharts and manage projects.

> ▸ Padlet (*padlet.com*)—group think/posting site; ask a question and collect people's thoughts in a unique way.

> ▸ Pixlr (*pixlr.com*)—Picture editing software to adjust and add special effects to an image. (The download is worth it!)

> ▸ Screen-Cast-O-Matic (*screencast-o-matic.com*)—Create a video of something you are doing on your computer; requires a download.

> ▸ ThingLink (*thinglink.com*)—Make images interactive then take a video of this!

> ▸ Vimeo (*vimeo.com*)—Video editing online; no download required.

> ▸ WeVideo (*wevideo.com*)—Editable, storage, video support.

> ▸ WordArt (*wordart.com*)—An online word art creator.

VII. **HOW THE ARTIFACT SUPPORTS YOUR EXPLORE PERFORMANCE TASK**

A. Your computational artifact is worth 20 percent of your Explore Performance Task score, and it is the first thing graders will see in this task. For you to get full credit, your artifact needs to:

1. tell an impactful story about the purpose, function, or effect of the innovation.

> *Your artifact is where you describe the innovation and its effect; it is not where you show your command of how to use the innovation. You do not need to own or be able to use the innovation to create an excellent artifact. You do need to show the impact that the innovation has on our world when it works as intended.*

2. be focused (related to the purpose, function, or effect of the innovation).

3. be created by you using a computer to do something that words cannot do.

B. To decide on the final artifact and the tools you will use, be sure to do the following:

1. Make sure your tools can create the artifact you are imagining.

   i. You had a creative vision for this artifact; be sure that the tools can support that vision.

   ii. Choose tools that can display the purpose, function, or effect of your innovation; be sure that the tools can do what you intended.

2. Make sure the innovation name is clearly visible.

3. Be sure that the function, purpose, and effect is clear in your artifact.

4. Keep the design clean and clear (simple backgrounds, neutral colors, etc.).

5. Be unique in your creation of an impactful artifact.

6. Ensure that your images and impact claims are cited and school-appropriate.

   i. Check your grammar.

   ii. Cite the source of any data or images that you are using.

   iii. Avoid violent or inappropriate images.

C. Keep in mind that the written response that is part of your Explore Performance Task is connected to the artifact in the following ways:

1. Prompts 2a and 2b focus on your digital artifact. (See Chapter 4 for further details.)

2. In your response to Prompt 2a, you:

    i. state the computing innovation.

    ii. describe the innovation's purpose and function.

    iii. explain how your artifact is showing a key aspect of your innovation.

3. In your response to Prompt 2b, you explain the steps you used to create this vision.

    i. It is here that you prove that you created your artifact by explaining the steps and tools you used.

    ii. Look at your response to 2b as an "artist's statement." This is how you clarify the story you are trying to tell about the innovation through your artifact.

4. In Prompts 2c and 2d, you will write about the effect of your innovation, and the data it uses. (See Chapters 5 and 6.)

5. In the final Prompt 2e, you will present your list of sources. (See Chapter 7.)

Written Responses Related to the Artifact
(Prompts 2a and 2b)

I. OVERVIEW

A. This chapter focuses on the part of your written responses in which you present and discuss your computational artifact. These will be your responses to Prompts 2a and 2b. In your response to Prompt 2a you will describe the vision behind your artifact, and in your response to Prompt 2b you will explain the process you used to create your computational artifact and answer questions about your research of the computing innovation you chose as your topic. Overall in the Explore Performance Task, you will be answering five prompts (2a through 2e). (See Chapters 5–7 for a discussion of the remaining Prompts 2c, 2d, and 2e.) All of these prompts are about both your artifact and the computing innovation you chose to research and display in the artifact.

B. Keep in mind the following when answering Prompts 2a through 2d:

   1. Use the template available from the College Board Digital Portfolio. Remember that you will need an authorized teacher's assistance to access the Digital Portfolio.

   2. Be sure that your written responses do not exceed 700 words for all four prompts.

      i. Stay below the maximum word count for each prompt.

      ii. The Digital Portfolio template counts words for you.

3. The references you will include in your response to Prompt 2e are *not* included in the word count. (See Chapter 7 for a discussion of Prompt 2e.)

C. Writing Prompts 2a and 2b focus on your digital artifact.

1. In responding to Prompt 2a, you explain your vision behind your artifact by:

    i. stating the computing innovation.

    ii. describing the innovation's purpose and function.

    iii. explaining how your artifact is showing the purpose, function, or effect of your innovation.

2. In responding to Prompt 2b, you prove you created your artifact by:

    i. explaining the steps you took to create this vision.

    ii. justifying why you chose the tool(s) you did to create this vision.

II. PROMPT 2a: EXPLAINING YOUR VISION

A. Prompt 2a asks you to provide information on your computing innovation and computational artifact. You have approximately 100 words to do the following:

1. Name the computing innovation that was your focus for your artifact and research.

2. Describe the innovation's intended purpose and function.

3. Describe how the artifact illustrates, represents, or explains the innovation's intended purpose, function, or effect.

Allow 30 minutes to 1 hour to name your innovation and explain its intended purpose and function. (Prompt 2a)

B. To maximize credit for Prompt 2a, do the following:

1. Remember the work you did to plan your artifact? Explain here what your artifact illustrates, represents, or explains.

2. Remember the questions and answers you had while researching? Explain the purpose, function, or effect your artifact highlights here.

3. Devote most of your words and time to the following:

   i.   Describe how the artifact illustrates, represents, or explains the innovation's intended purpose, function, or effect.

   ii. Explain your vision for your artifact. Be specific. Use the words *illustrate*, *represent*, or *explain* in your response. *One* of the following questions needs to be answered to get full credit:

   ▸ What does your artifact *illustrate* about your computing innovation?

   ▸ What does your artifact *represent* about your computing innovation?

   ▸ What does your artifact *explain* about your computing innovation?

   iii. Connect to the innovation's intended purpose, function, or effect. Use the words *purpose*, *function*, or *effect* in your response. *One* of the following questions needs to be answered to get full credit:

   ▸ How does the artifact reveal, represent, or explain the intended *purpose* of your computing innovation?

   ▸ How does the artifact reveal, represent, or explain the *function* of your computing innovation?

   ▸ How does the artifact reveal, represent, or explain the *effect* of your computing innovation?

Look at your response to Prompt 2a as your "Vision Statement" for your Explore Performance Task. This is your chance to explain how the artifact showcases the function, purpose, or effect of the computational innovation you chose as your topic. Here you are the artist explaining how your artwork brings the entire task together.

III. PROMPT 2b: TAKING CREDIT FOR YOUR PROCESS

A. Prompt 2b asks you for a description of the process you used to develop your artifact. This prompt is how you prove that you created your artifact. You have approximately 100 words to do the following:

1. Identify the computing tools and techniques you used.

2. Provide enough detail so the grader understands the work you did (creative and computational) to create your artifact.

3. Explain how the tool or technique helped you to create your artifact.

Allow 30 minutes to 1 hour to describe the processes you used to develop your artifact. (Prompt 2b)

B. For Prompt 2b, do the following:

1. In one or two sentences, state the tools and techniques you used.

   i.   Avoid jargon and acronyms.

   ii. To help you state this simply, imagine you are explaining what you did to an elementary school student.

2. Devote most of your words and time to explaining your development process. Here are some tips to maximize your score in this part:

   i.   Do not connect to the innovation here unless it is related to the process.

   ii. Remember the work you did to learn about the tools you could use to create your artifact? Use this prompt to take credit for that work.

   iii. Answer the following questions about your development process to create your computational artifact:

   ▸ What tools did you use for your artifact? (In your response, use the word *tools,* and connect to your *plan* for your artifact.)

   ▸ Why did you use these tools? What made these tools a good fit for the story you were trying to tell?

   ▸ What did you do to make these tools work?

   ▸ How did you learn that you had to do this? (Use the word *techniques* in your response.)

Written Response
Related to Effect
(Prompt 2c)

Allow about 2 hours to complete explaining the effect your innovation has had or will have. (Prompt 2c)

I. PROMPT 2c

A. Prompt 2c asks you to explain, in 250 words or less, the effect your innovation has had, or has the potential to have. To get full credit for this prompt, use your research to:

1. explain one beneficial effect directly caused by your computing innovation.

2. explain one harmful effect directly caused by your computing innovation.

3. connect the beneficial effect to a current or future impact to society, culture, or the economy.

4. connect the harmful effect to a current or future impact to society, culture, or the economy.

250 words is not a lot of words! Plan your words carefully, and use research to justify every claim you make. Remember, your effect needs to be specifically connected to the innovation you defined in your response to Prompt 2a. Do more research if you need more information to make a full response.

B. To maximize your score on Prompt 2c, do the following:

1. Connect the important facts of your response to your research.

   i. Use numerical superscripts that correspond with your references to make it easy for your grader to find your citations.

   ii. Your citations that you will list later in your answer to Prompt 2e do not need to be alphabetized.

   ▸ Common ways to organize citations are to put them in the order that they appear in the task, or in the order that you found them while researching.

   iii. When you researched this task, you should have saved each full citation and kept a numbered list of all citations.

   ▸ If you have not created a list of citations, take the time now to make a list of all your sources.

   ▸ Use an accepted citation format right from the start so you won't have to do this later when you respond to Prompt 2e.

2. Follow the steps below to state and prove a harmful effect of the innovation you chose. You will need to prove one harmful effect caused by your innovation.

Test Tip

Remember from Chapter 2 that there are two main ways to prove an effect. For a summary of these two approaches, see Approach 1 and Approach 2 below.

   i. First, state the effect.

   ▸ Remember, the effect needs to impact more people than just those who own the innovation.

   ▸ The effect on a society, economy, or culture should be caused by the innovation working as intended.

    ii. Include the words *harmful effect* to make your response easy to find.

    iii. Then, use one of the following approaches to prove the effect:

- Approach 1 (most direct): You found research that proves your computational innovation directly caused a harm to an entire culture, a society (which could be as small as a group of close friends), or an economy.

- Approach 2 (requires more research, which is likely if your innovation is new): You found research on an older computing innovation that is very similar to your computing innovation. Using the older innovation, prove that this innovation caused harm to an entire culture, a society, or an economy.

3. State and prove a beneficial effect. As was the case with the harmful effect claim, use one of the two approaches:

    i. Approach 1: Cite the research you found that directly connects your innovation to a beneficial effect in terms of a culture, a society, or an economy. Remember:

- State effects that are caused by the innovation working as intended.

- State impacts on those who do not own or use the innovation.

    ii. Approach 2: Find a parallel innovation that has enough in common with your innovation that you can make valid claims about likely benefits. Use this approach if you are having difficulty finding research that connects directly to your innovation.

Test Tip

Help readers to find your response by including the words **benefit** *and* **harm** *in the sentences that you are writing about effect. Instead of using words that suggest benefit, be explicit by writing: "One beneficial effect of my innovation is . . . ." Then, prove your point with the statement and the citation.*

II. **FINALIZING YOUR WRITTEN RESPONSE TO PROMPT 2c**

A. When you read your final written response, be sure you are able to answer "yes" to each of the following questions. If not, revise your response to maximize your score.

B. Below are the questions that graders will ask themselves when they read your response to decide if you should earn full credit for your response.

Question	Yes	No
Did you provide an example of a beneficial effect?		
Using research, did you prove that this beneficial effect was caused by your computing innovation working as intended?		
Using research, did you prove that this effect was beneficial and show the impact on one of the following: a society, a culture, or an economy?		
Using research, did you justify why the effect on society, culture, or economy was a benefit even to those who do not own or use the innovation?		
Did you provide an example of a harmful effect?		
Using research, did you prove that this harmful effect was caused by your computing innovation working as intended?		
Using research, did you prove that this effect was harmful and show the impact on one of the following: a society, a culture, or an economy?		
Using research, did you justify why the effect on society, culture, or economy was a concern even to those who do not own or use the innovation?		

Written Response Related to Data
(Prompt 2d)

It should take you between 1 and 2 hours to describe the data your innovation uses and a data concern.

I. PROMPT 2d

A. Prompt 2d asks you to focus on the data used, produced, or transformed by the innovation you defined in Prompt 2a. This prompt needs to be completed using 250 words or less. To get full credit for this prompt, use your research to:

1. Describe the data your computing innovation uses.

2. Choose *one* of the following:

   i.   Explain how the innovation consumes data (as input).

   ii. Explain how the innovation produces data (as output).

   iii. Explain how the innovation transforms data.

3. Show that you considered where the data in your innovation may be vulnerable by detailing a concern in *one* of the following areas:

   i.   data storage

   ii. data privacy

   iii. data security

The data you want to write about in this prompt is the data that is consumed, produced, or transformed by the innovation. To find this data, research how the data becomes binary digits or bits. The data could be a sound file, a graphics file, binary data, an electrical current, etc. It depends on your innovation and what your research tells you.

B. To maximize your score on Prompt 2d, do the following:

1. Verify that your research meets the requirements for this prompt.

   i.   Your research should help you to determine what data you will focus on in your response to this prompt.

   ii. You are looking for data that satisfies each of the following:

   - The data is input, transformed, and output from your computing innovation.

   - You can find evidence of a data security, data storage, or data privacy concern.

   - The data is reduced to a type such as an integer or number, Boolean, text, image, video, audio, or signal.

Data collection devices are examples of hardware; they are not data. For example, in a self-driving car, sensors are used to collect data. The sensors themselves are not data. Data is something that a computer can process. So, for this example, images would be an example of data.

   iii. If your current research does not provide some type of information that is processed by a computer, do more research.

   iv. Use numerical superscripts that correspond to your references.

   v. Save the citations to a separate file. To simplify your compilation of sources:

      ▸ make a numbered list of the citations, and add each new source to this list as you find it.

      ▸ use any acceptable citation format (MLA, APA, etc.) from the start.

2. Identify key parts of what data looks like for your computing innovation. To maximize credit for this part of the prompt, you need to:

   i. state the data that will be the focus of your written response.

      ▸ Include the word *data* in your response.

      ▸ Connect data to your research. (This can be accomplished in one sentence.)

   ii. investigate the data until you can explain the type of data being stored, processed, and transformed.

      ▸ The data type needs to be clear.

      ▸ Use a few sentences to explain how the innovation changes the data from user input (which could be a person or a machine) to binary digits that are processed by your innovation.

      ▸ To find these steps during your research, search "data transformations *and* your innovation name."

   iii. Explain how this data is consumed, produced, or transformed.

      ▸ Use "according to" statements or superscripts to connect this statement to your research.

▸ Clarify which part of the data's path you will focus on. Use the words *consumed, transformed,* or *produced* in your response. This should be completed in two to three sentences.

3. Write about data concerns for your computing innovation. To maximize credit for this part of the prompt, remember to:

   i. state the concern using the words *data privacy, data storage,* or *data security* to clarify your response.

   ii. prove that the concern is related to your computing innovation by citing research.

   iii. explain why the identified concern is an issue. To earn full credit, be sure you identify:

      ▸ who will be impacted by this concern.

      ▸ what could happen to an individual or a larger group if this concern is not addressed.

      ▸ why this concern is caused by the innovation stated in Prompt 2a.

II. **FINALIZING YOUR WRITTEN RESPONSE TO PROMPT 2d**

A. When you read your final written response, be sure you are able to answer "yes" to each of the following questions. If not, revise your response to maximize your score. These are the questions that graders will ask themselves when they read your response to decide if you should earn full credit for your response.

Question	Yes	No
Did you identify the data that your computing innovation uses?		
Did you prove that this data is part of your innovation by connecting this claim to research?		
Did you reduce the data to a type that is processed by a computer by your computing innovation, and did you explain this?		

Question	Yes	No
Did you explain how this data is consumed, produced, or transformed by your innovation?		
Did you prove how the data is consumed, produced, or transformed by connecting this claim to research?		
Did you identify a storage, privacy, or security concern for this data?		
Did you prove this concern by connecting this claim to research?		
Did you explain what could happen as a result of this concern?		

Completing Your Explore Performance Task
(Prompt 2e)

Congratulations! If you are reading this chapter, you are close to finishing your Explore Performance Task.

This chapter focuses on the final steps for submitting your Explore Performance Task, which include:

1. your citations (Prompt 2e).

2. preparing documents to be submitted.

3. using the Digital Portfolio.

> Allow 1 to 2 hours to organize your sources and submit your Explore Performance Task to the College Board.

I. ORGANIZING YOUR RESPONSE TO PROMPT 2e

A. Prompt 2e asks you to provide a list of all online or print sources you used to create and/or support your responses to the prompts regarding your computational artifact. The list you provide in response to this prompt does **not** count against your word count.

B. To get full credit for Prompt 2e, do the following:

1. Cite at least three sources. At least two of the sources listed must have been created after the end of the previous academic year.

   i.   Your citations for online sources require the information listed below. Most of this information is public. If you have trouble finding any of it, try searching for the URL of your source on the website *whois.com*. If any information listed below is not available, omit it in your response.

> ▸ The permanent URL
>
> ▸ Author
>
> ▸ Title of site
>
> ▸ Source (Who is responsible for this URL? This could be a person or a company.)
>
> ▸ Date retrieved
>
> ▸ Date reference was written or posted

  ii.   Print sources require the following information:

> ▸ Author
>
> ▸ Title of excerpt/article and magazine or book
>
> ▸ Page number(s)
>
> ▸ Publisher
>
> ▸ Date of publication

 iii.   Interview sources require the following information:

> ▸ Name of person interviewed
>
> ▸ Date on which interview occurred
>
> ▸ Person's position

2. Note that each source should be numbered, relevant, credible, and easily accessed.

Test Tip

There is no word or page count limit for this prompt, so take the time to make a clear presentation. Consider creating two sections. Title the first section "Citations Related to Artifact," and title the second section "Citations in Written Responses."

II. CONVERTING FILES TO FINAL VERSIONS BEFORE SUBMITTING

A. You will need to submit two pieces of your Explore Performance Task to the College Board:

1. Your computational artifact

2. Your written responses

B. Keep in mind these important details about the computational artifact.

1. Remember, your artifact can be any one of the following:

    i.   A video or audio file that is less than 1 minute in length and under 30 MB in size.

    ii. A PDF that is less than three pages.

2. The artifact must be saved with one of the following file extensions: *.mp3, .mp4, .wmv, .avi, .mov, .wav, .aif, or .pdf.*

    i.   To find the file extension, look at the properties of the file.

    ii. If the file is a document, convert it to print as a PDF.

    iii. If the file is a video or audio file, use your video or audio editor to convert the file to an appropriate file type. If this is not possible, find an online tool that you can use to convert the file.

3. The artifact needs to clearly state your computing innovation.

4. If you used outside sources for any part of the artifact, cite these sources in Prompt 2e. Put superscripts on the artifact or explain in Prompt 2e where these sources were used.

C. Keep in mind these important details about your written responses.

    1. Use the College Board template so that Prompts 2a through 2e are shown and your responses appear below each prompt.

    2. After you have entered your responses into the template, you will need to convert the template to a PDF for submission.

As a final check, refer to Appendix E for your Explore Performance Task checklist. This checklist summarizes the key requirements based on the latest Scoring Guidelines.

III. USING THE DIGITAL PORTFOLIO TO SUBMIT YOUR TASK

A. Before you press the "Final Submit" button on your Digital Portfolio, spend some time making sure you are maximizing your score. Be sure you can answer "yes" to each of these questions:

Prompt	Requirement	Yes	No
1	Does your artifact illustrate, represent, or explain the computing innovation's purpose, function, or effect?		
1, 2a	Does your artifact identify the innovation?		
2a	Did you identify and state a plausible fact about the innovation's purpose or function?		
2b	Was your artifact created using a computational tool?		
2b	Did you explain how you created the artifact well enough so anyone can understand?		
2c	Did you identify a beneficial effect of the innovation?		
2c	Did you identify a harmful effect of the innovation?		

(continued)

Prompt	Requirement	Yes	No
2c	Did you explain how these effects impact a society, a culture, or an economy?		
2d	Did you identify the data that the innovation uses?		
2d	Did you explain how the innovation consumes, produces, or transforms data?		
2d	Did you identify **one** data storage, data privacy, or data security concern in this computing innovation? (Be sure the concern is connected to the innovation.)		
2d	Did you explain how the data storage, data privacy, or data security concern could harm an individual or larger group?		
2e	Do you provide online citations of at least three sources?		
2e	Are these citations used in your written responses (with superscripts or "according to" phrasing)?		
	Did you check your word counts? Keep the word count within the specified guidelines. The template provided by College Board will do this for you.		

B. When you are ready, follow these steps to submit:

1. Communicate with the teacher who is your school point of contact and let him/her know you plan to submit your task.

2. Go to *digitalportfolio.collegeboard.org* and log in.

3. Find your class and click on the Explore Performance Task.

4. Follow directions to upload your artifact.

   ▸ The site will prompt you to check the version you are uploading.

   ▸ Upload your artifact.

   ▸ Verify that this is the version you want to submit. Then, either submit this version, or upload a different version.

5. Follow directions to upload your written responses (Prompts 2a–2e). Again, you will be prompted to verify that this is your final version.

Celebrate! You have just submitted the Explore Performance Task, which will become 16 percent of your AP Computer Science Principles score. Take a moment to reflect on all that you've learned.

Your next step is the Create Performance Task, where *you* are the main innovator.

PART II

THE CREATE PERFORMANCE TASK

Introduction to the Create Performance Task

I. OVERVIEW

A. The Create Performance Task is worth 24 percent of your AP Computer Science Principles score. This performance task consists of the following three parts:

1. Designing and creating a program

2. Debugging and testing the program

3. Documenting the program

B. When you finish the Create Performance Task, you will submit the following three items to the College Board via the Digital Portfolio:

1. A video of your program running a significant feature that you coded.

2. A PDF of your responses to written Prompts 2a through 2d.

3. A PDF of your entire program code.

C. The Create Performance Task should take about 12 hours to complete. If you work 45 minutes per day on this task, it should take you about 15–16 days to finish. If, however, you decide to use a programming language you don't know, the task could take significantly longer.

D. This task, along with the Explore Performance Task (see Chapters 2–7), needs to be completed and submitted to the College Board using the Digital Portfolio by April 30.

II. ABOUT THE CREATE PERFORMANCE TASK

A. The Create Performance Task is your chance to use a programming language to create something new.

B. The Create Performance Task can be done collaboratively, but a significant part of the code must be designed and implemented individually.

C. Be sure to read the information about both the Create Performance Task itself and the scoring guidelines, which are available at AP Central (*apcentral.collegeboard.org*).

D. To maximize your score, be sure to respond to each prompt clearly, and always cite any source to which you refer.

E. There are three parts to this performance task:

1. Creating your program.

2. Explaining your program.

3. Documenting your program.

III. HOW THE CREATE PERFORMANCE TASK RELATES TO THE SOFTWARE DEVELOPMENT CYCLE

A. To excel on the Create Performance Task, you will need to go through the usual stages of the Software Development Cycle. You must accomplish each of the four steps to complete the cycle. (We will discuss the first two steps of the Software Development Cycle in this chapter and the final two steps in Chapter 9.)

Steps of the Software Development Cycle

Step 1: IDEA

Decide your vision for your program.
- Will you solve a problem?
- Will you learn something new?
- Will you create something with your program?
- Will you replicate a behavior?
- Will you generate a tool for others to use?

Step 2: DESIGN

Decide on the approach you will use for your program. Flowcharts, pseudocode, or some other visual mapping of your plan is common in this step.

Step 3: IMPLEMENT

Write your program based on your design.

Step 4: TEST

Fix what is not working to align your program with your idea.

IV. **HOW TO MAXIMIZE YOUR SCORE**

A. Brainstorm about a program.

1. Brainstorming about an idea for your program is part of Step 1 of the Software Development Cycle.

The Brainstorming/Idea phase is part of the "create" phase of this project. The amount of time it takes is different for everyone. Be sure to decide on a time limit for this phase of the project.

2. Your program is the center of your Create Performance Task. The program must demonstrate:

   i. Use of math and logic that shows your programming skills.

   ii. Creation and use of complex algorithms based on math and logical concepts.

   iii. Development and use of abstractions to manage the complexity of your program.

You'll need about 6 hours to complete the steps of the Create Performance Task outlined in Chapters 8 and 9. If you need to learn a new programming language, you'll need to allow more time.

3. When thinking about what program to write, focus on creating a program that means something to you.

4. Here are some questions to ask yourself to help generate ideas about the program you decide to create:

   i. What programming language do I know well?

   ii. What behavior would I like to create in my program?

   iii. What game would I like to simulate?

   iv. What is the purpose I would like my program to fulfill?

   v. What problem would I like to solve with mys program?

   vi. What could I build with my programming skill?

5. While brainstorming, consider extending a project you have already worked on. By the time you are ready to submit it, the project will most likely look quite different from its original form.

6. Decide if your brainstormed idea will put you in a good position to answer written responses. Your written responses will be your opportunity to explain:

   i. the development process of your program, including difficulties and opportunities.

ii. an important set of algorithms and how they work together and independently to serve a function in your program.

iii. an important abstraction and how it manages complexity in your program.

Although you need to submit your program code for your Create Performance Task, your score for this performance task depends mostly on your written responses to the prompts about your contributions to the code.

7. You will know that you have a good idea for your program if you can answer "yes" to each of the following questions:

Question	Yes	No
Is your idea interesting to you?		
Can you see how your idea can be accomplished using a language that you know, or one that you plan to learn and use?		
Is your idea complex enough that multiple lines of code will be needed and that the order of these lines will be important?		
Is your idea complex enough that you will have repeated behaviors that should be coded using a procedure or method?		
Is your idea complex enough that you can see how planning before you start coding will help you?		
Is your idea complex enough that you will need a collection or a list?		
Is your idea complex enough that you will need to iterate through a collection or use a loop in another way?		

B. Decide on Your Programming Language

1. Next you need to decide on the language you will use to solve a problem, study something new, or express yourself. You need a language that allows you to:

    i.   create variables that can hold different data types such as strings, integers, floating point numbers (or doubles).

    ii. create collections (also called lists or arrays).

    iii. control sequence and selection.

        ▸ Order matters.

        ▸ You can have as many lines of code as you choose.

        ▸ Use and create conditional statements such as *if, else if,* or *else* to control logical flow of decisions in code.

    iv. control names of key parts of code—this will make it easier to explain what they do in the written portion of this task.

    v.   repeat (iteration).

        ▸ You can do the same thing repeatedly using loops like *while* or *for* loops.

        ▸ You can use these loops to move through a list.

    vi. create procedures or methods which is helpful when behavior is significant and/or repeated in a program.

    vii. create abstractions.

        ▸ These could be a procedure or an object.

        ▸ These are helpful when a characteristic needs to be repeated or managed in code.

2. Decide on the amount of learning you will need to do to finish your program. (See Appendix B for a partial list of programming languages that meet the requirements for this task.)

    i.   If your school or teacher has chosen a language for your class, it is often easiest to complete this task with that language. Keep in mind, however, that this language may not be the best fit for what you hope to do with your program.

ii. If you do not have a lot of experience with programming, all of the languages listed in Appendix B have considerable resources and support online. Remember, however, that not all of these languages are a good fit for a first-time programmer.

iii. At this point reflect on the following:

▸ Spend some time looking over resources.

▸ Think about what you hope to create.

▸ Consider how much time you can devote to learning.

iv. Use this table to organize your thoughts.

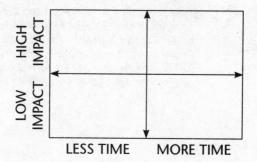

▸ This is a 2 × 2 decision matrix. These matrices are useful for making a decision when you need to weigh more than one option at a time.

▸ In this case, use this matrix as a way to organize weighing time required versus the impact of your program on whoever will use your program.

▸ Use this matrix throughout this task to decide if any change to your code is worth the time required to complete it.

▸ Often the "ideal" plan will put you in the top left box. In this area of the matrix, your plan would be accomplished in a reasonable amount of time, but it would also impact your user(s).

3. If you decide to learn a new language, start learning right away.

   i.   Search to find resources. Many resources are free and come with support communities with online blogs, tutorials, or even in-person meetings.

   ii.   See Appendix B for links to the main site for each language, related downloads, and help.

   iii. Expect that you might need to add several more hours to the time needed to complete the entire Create Performance Task.

Test Tip

Take some time to check out the Create Performance Task samples in the "Sample Responses to Performance Tasks" area on AP Central (apcentral.collegeboard.org). The College Board has collected samples of work completed by students just like you and provided their score and feedback to help you understand how your score will be determined.

C. Design Your Solution

1. Now that you have brainstormed about an idea and decided which programming language to use, it's time to decide how to manage this idea and design your solution. We'll now explore step 2 of the Software Development Cycle, Design. In this step, you will decide on the approach you want to use for your program. Flowcharts, pseudocode, or another visual mapping of your plan are common in this step.

2. Here are the likely decisions and recommended steps to designing a great solution.

   i.   One of your first decisions is: Will I do this project independently or in collaboration with another programmer? There are benefits (and drawbacks) to each approach.

ii. Consider the following points if you think you would like to work with someone else:

- ▸ Benefits:
  - – You will probably do something together that is much larger than what each of you can do alone.
  - – You will have help at each phase—brainstorming, coding, and debugging.
  - – You will hear another person's ideas and see another person's approach.

- ▸ To make success likely, you will need to communicate and evaluate your abilities and the abilities of the person you are considering working with on this project. For example, if the two of you are not equally strong in coding, decide if your weaknesses complement your partner's strengths, and vice versa.
  - – Example of complementary skills: You are very good with graphics and image editing, but you are a beginning programmer. Your partner is very strong with data storage and programming, but weak using image editors.
  - – Example of skills that may not work well for this project: You are both good at graphics and image editing. You are both starting to learn how to program. This could be a problem because it would be difficult for you to learn from each other.
  - – To improve your chances for a successful partnership, you want the skills of each partner to be unique so you can help each other grow. The best partnerships for this task have complementary skills.

- ▸ Begin thinking and deciding about how to divide the work. Each of you will need to write enough code so that you each write your own responses to the performance task. You will need to indicate the code you wrote and the code your partner wrote. There are two ways to manage this:

- You and your partner work collaboratively on a single program based on your shared idea. Then, you break apart so you can each handle your own independent ideas.

- You each start out with different ideas, but you find that you run into similar problems as you code. You then help each other find solutions for how to improve the design, debug, and test the code.

- You might need to meet many times per week to accomplish this task while you are coding. This could be done using video conferencing as long as you are both comfortable with this tool.

- You need to agree on how to share code ahead of time. Dropbox, Google Team Drives or Shared Folders, or GitHub are commonly used if face-to-face work is inconvenient.

iii. Consider the following points if you think you would like to do this task independently:

▸ Benefits:

- You do not need to meet with someone else on a regular basis.

- You can focus on your idea.

- If you learn well independently, you can spend more time learning about how to improve your project.

▸ To make success likely:

- Planning is essential. Develop weekly goals for yourself, including the amount of time you will spend on the project and what you hope to accomplish.

     – Take frequent breaks. It is often better to work for 1 or 2 hours, do something else, and then return to your project.

3. Whether or not you are planning to work with another person, you should use concrete tools to manage your design.

V. TIPS FOR DESIGN

A. At a minimum, your design should answer the following questions:

1. Where does your program start and end?

2. Where will key decisions be made?

3. Which decisions need to happen in order, and what is that order?

4. What is the input needed at key steps?

5. What is the output you expect at key steps?

6. What behaviors or processes are being repeated? (These are great candidates for procedures.)

7. How will the functionality of the program be managed and procedures called? (This is where your algorithms will be implemented.)

VI. TOOLS FOR DESIGNING

A. There are many tools that will help you design your program. Choose the tool that best meets your needs.

1. Flowchart on paper.

    i. Your first design should be on paper unless you and your partner are very comfortable using computer-based tools.

ii. If paper-and-pencil is not working, consider using a whiteboard and markers.

iii. Start practicing with the symbols below. You will see these on your End-of-Course Exam.

Flowchart Symbol	Meaning
OVAL	Indicates the beginning or end of a program.
ARROW	Shows relationships between parts of code; represents flow of information and/or logical path of code.
PARALLELOGRAM	Shows input or output of a program; could be data or text.
RECTANGLE	Indicates key step in logic that has one input and one output.
RHOMBUS	Shows a key decision; may be more than one input. Output will be Boolean (which can only be true or false).

2. If you are collaborating virtually with another person, or if you are comfortable using computer-based tools, here are some online tools that may help:

   i. Online Flowchart Maker (*draw.io*) — Create simple flowcharts and share these charts easily via Drive, OneDrive, GitHub, Dropbox, or to your device.

   ii. MindMeister (*mindmeister.com*) — Create more complicated flowcharts and manage projects. This online tool is free and easy to use. It is ideal when you are trying to work with another person on a large project.

iii. Padlet (*padlet.com*)—Create a wall to organize your thoughts, videos, links, and ideas with another person or independently.

VII. MAINTAINING YOUR DESIGN

A. Whether you decide to make your flowchart on paper or use one of the computer-based tools, keep your design close by. Modify it frequently to be sure you are processing how any change will influence the entire program.

1. A flowchart is a great way for teams to communicate. It also helps people working alone remember key decisions that they made along the way.

2. Take pictures or use a snipping tool to capture an image of each version of your design. Include words to explain why you made these changes. These thoughts and images will help you later when you draft your written responses to the prompts.

VIII. COMPLETING YOUR FIRST JOURNAL ENTRY

A. Now you will begin the essential job of keeping a journal documenting your work throughout the Create Performance Task by making your first journal entry, which will concern your design. It is essential to document your initial design because the overall design will change for many reasons as you code. You will need to write about all these changes in your written responses later. A few things to keep in mind about this journal:

i. It is essential to keep a journal for the Create Performance Task because it may take you many weeks of coding before you are ready to complete the written portion of this task.

ii. Think of your design and all the changes to it as you write your journal entries for your Create Performance Task. Document all of these changes as you go along.

    iii. In your responses to the performance task prompts that you will write later, you will need to explain decisions made during these weeks. Your journal will ensure that you remember them all.

B. Your journal can be managed in many ways. You may choose to use paper, a word processor, or another tool you prefer. Regardless of how you manage it, your journal should be your own.

    i. Keep an independent journal, even if you are working with someone else. It will be good material for you to use later when you will need to write and submit your own written responses to prompts about your part of the program.

    ii. Write your journal from your own perspective. Writing down your thoughts will help you remember what you were thinking throughout this project.

C. If any of the following things happen while you are coding, you should stop coding and write about it in your journal:

    i. You changed your design to improve the function or readability of your code.

    ii. You figured out a better way to code something.

    iii. You had help from someone else to figure something out.

    iv. You modified your design based on someone else's feedback.

D. When you write a journal entry, you should include as many of the following details as possible:

    i. Date of journal entry

    ii. If someone helped you, who was it?

       ▸ What did this person do to help you?

       ▸ What did you learn from this help?

iii. If you found something online, where did you find it?

- ▶ Cite this source completely while you have the link. This will save you time later!

- ▶ What did this source have that was helpful?

- ▶ What did you learn from this source?

iv. Image of your design

- ▶ If you changed something in your design, what was it?

v. If you added a procedure, what did you add and why?

- ▶ What behavior will it help you to control?

- ▶ What will it help you to manage?

- ▶ Does it have a collection (list, array)?

- ▶ Does it use a loop (*for*, *while*)?

- ▶ Does it have conditional statements (*if*, *else*)?

- ▶ Were any parameters used or needed?

Now that you have an idea, a design, and an approach for how to journal changes to your design and learning, you are ready to program.

Creating Your Program

Allow about 6 hours to complete the portion of the Create Performance Task covered in this chapter. This time includes the steps already accomplished in Chapter 8.

I. OVERVIEW

A. At this point you should have completed the following actions in your Create Performance Task:

1. You have decided on a programming language. (See Appendix B for ideas and links, or Chapter 8 for more explanation.)

2. You are familiar enough with this language so that you can:

   i.   define a variable.

   ii.   create a string, integer, floating point, and a list of variables.

   iii. receive input from a user and give output to a user.

   iv.   write conditional statements (*if, else-if, else*).

   v.   write loops (*for, while*).

   vi.   define procedures (code that is called by lines of code in the program or by the user of the program).

3. You have an idea for your task. (See Chapter 8.)

4. You have started your journal. (See Chapter 8.)

II. UNDERSTAND HOW YOUR PROGRAM SUPPORTS YOUR CREATE PERFORMANCE TASK

A. The planning and work that you do to create your final program is part of each question that you will answer for your Create Performance Task.

B. To get full credit, your Create Performance Task submission needs to show that you completed all of the following accomplishments:

1. You did what you planned to do. This means one of the following:

   i. You solved the problem you set out to solve.

   ii. You "taught" your computer to do something using a program that you could not do before the program.

   iii. You expressed a personal interest using the program as your tool.

2. You used approaches to design that show you can answer the following questions about your code design choices:

   i. Data Types—How are you going to store and process the data used by your program? What data type would make the data easy to store, read, and transform?

   ii. Logic—Why did the order matter for those blocks of code? What did a loop do for you in your program? How are particular blocks of code selected for execution?

   iii. Conditional Statements—Why did you need to check the truth of that statement first? What does *else* mean in your program?

   iv. Procedures—What behavior is being handled through this procedure? Why is it helping you in your program?

   v. Abstractions—How are you managing the complexity of your code?

C. Keep in mind that your Create Performance Task write-up is connected to the program in the following ways:

1. In Prompt 1, you submit a video that demonstrates the running of at least one significant feature in your program.

> *If you choose to highlight a feature that you coded in your video, it will make explaining the feature more straightforward.*

2. In Prompt 2a, you state the programming language used, define the purpose of your program, and explain the function of the program.

3. In Prompt 2b, you describe both the incremental and iterative processes you went through to create your program and you address difficulties, opportunities, and resolutions that occurred during this process.

4. In Prompt 2c, you show and write about an algorithm that *you* created that was fundamental to your program. This algorithm needs to:

    i.   integrate other algorithms.

    ii. show use of mathematical or logical concepts by showing you understand the importance of the order and sequencing of code; the use of conditionals to control this order; and how loops help to manage repeated code.

    iii. be related to the main purpose of the program.

5. In Prompt 2d, you show and write about an abstraction that you developed. This abstraction needs to:

    i.   show you understand that order matters and how to use conditionals and loops in your code.

    ii. show the use of math and logic.

    iii. be used in your program to manage complexity.

6. In Prompt 2e, you show all of the code that makes your program run. Here you will need to:

    i.   put an oval around the algorithm you wrote about in 2c.

    ii.   put a rectangle around the abstraction you wrote about in 2d.

    iii.   include comments or citations for code written by someone else.

D. Keep the following in mind: as you work through this task remember that your program is the center of your Create Performance Task and that it is important that you have a plan in place to manage your time.

III. IMPLEMENTING AND TESTING YOUR PROGRAM WITH INCREMENTAL AND ITERATIVE CHANGES

A. Now you are in the third and fourth steps of the Software Development Cycle as you implement and test your solutions. The first two steps were discussed in Chapter 8. As you recall, these two steps were:

1. Step 1: IDEA—Deciding your vision for your program.

2. Step 2: DESIGN—Deciding on your approach for your program.

You are now ready to take on the final two steps in the Software Development cycle:

3. Step 3: IMPLEMENT—Write your program based on your design.

4. Step 4: TEST—Fix what is not working to align your program with your idea for what you hoped this program would do.

(If you move back to step 1 of the Software Development Cycle because of a change in your idea, you will probably need to redesign as well.)

When you code, it is important that you test the code as you write it. It is recommended that you code 1–2 lines (or blocks) at a time then test to be sure your code is working as you expect. This is called incremental testing. The amount of time you spend debugging will increase if you write more code and do not perform incremental tests.

B. Up until now, the development of your performance task has been described in a linear way. First, you have an idea; then you design, then you implement, and finally, you test. This is an incremental approach to programming.

INCREMENTAL DESIGN MODEL

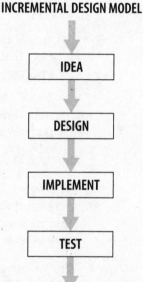

C. In reality, completing this task will be both *incremental* and *iterative*. It's important to understand the difference between these two approaches because you will need to write about both of them in the written portion of your Create Performance Task.

D. An *incremental* change is based on design. Incremental changes tend to be larger and connected to a plan you put together before coding. Be sure to use the word "incremental" to describe these types of changes.

During the June 2017 grading, AP submissions for the Create Performance Task showed that writing about iterative and incremental changes to code was challenging. It is worth practicing this and checking with a partner to see if your explanations are clear.

E. An *iterative* change is often caused by, or happens during, a repeated run through this cycle.

1. All of the following are examples of iterative changes:

    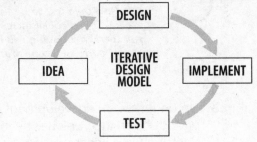

    i. You changed your design to improve your code.

    ii. You added a new feature to improve the functionality of your program.

    iii. Through coding, you learned you needed something (a new requirement) that was not included in your initial plan. You added that while coding.

2. Iterative changes are smaller and tested more often.

3. When you start programming, the first step is often incremental since you would be writing code based on a design. Your exact process depends on how unusual the language or design is for you.

4. The longer people code in a language, the more comfortable they tend to be with iterative changes.

5. The more complicated a program, the more you will see both incremental and iterative changes become necessary.

F. In large projects, there is greater need for:

   i. organization.

   ii. recording changes (in case something stops working or you have to explain why you made a change).

   iii. design (in general, the time spent on design grows in proportion to the project).

IV. **A GENERAL PLAN FOR MANAGING YOUR TIME**

A. Once you know a language and have your design plan, the most challenging part of the Create Performance Task is managing your time. This section assumes that you:

    i. know a programming language.

    ii. have an idea and a design.

    iii. are ready to devote time to writing your program.

B. Implementing a program requires flexibility. Changes are common. However, if you decide to change a key idea for your program or a major piece of your design, you may need more time than is shown here.

Hour	Goals	Managing Common Issues	Additional Information that Should Be in Your Journal*
1	You started writing code to align with the structure you used in your design. Some programmers code the beginning (main input) and the end first. Others code from the beginning to the next major section.	You realize that your design does not have enough detail. To solve this, add details to the design until you can write code.	What do you like about your design? What are major challenges in your design and how will you fix this? What incremental or iterative changes have happened? If other people helped you, write about this.
2	You complete the structure. Methods or procedures might be missing their bodies, but they are being called where they should be. The order makes sense and aligns with your design.	You focus on writing one method or debugging one thing. To solve this, try to step away from the code and focus on your design.	What section of code will you choose to write about in Prompt 2c? You need to create an algorithm that calls other algorithms and uses math and logic (sequence, selection, iteration).

(continued)

* See the end of Chapter 8 to review what needs to be included in your journal entries.

Hour	Goals	Managing Common Issues	Additional Information that Should Be in Your Journal
3	Write and test the algorithm that will be your focus in the write-up. Name your algorithm something that is meaningful in your program. Be sure it is complex enough. It should: – call other algorithms; – contain sequencing, selection, and iteration.	You find a bug in the algorithm through testing. To solve this, use debugging tools you learned with your programming language.	How does this algorithm connect to the purpose and function of your program? What other algorithms do you need to write?
4	Write other algorithms. Be on the lookout for repeated code that might become an abstraction. Test your code frequently.	You have written several lines of code and waited to test. Now you cannot tell where the issue came from in your code. To solve this, comment out code you created in order until you have only 2–3 lines of code to test. Then test and fix 2–3 lines at a time.	If you have not had a difficulty or an opportunity working with your code, you should work toward this end. Learn something new, then use it in your code. What will you do for your abstraction? Note that this could be your procedure that you created during Hour 3.

Hour	Goals	Managing Common Issues	Additional Information that Should Be in Your Journal
5	Write an abstraction that meets the following requirements or verify that the procedure that you wrote in Hour 3 meets the following requirements: – The abstraction uses sequence, selection, iteration, logic, and at least one math concept. – The abstraction manages complexity by removing repeated code or managing a complex task.	You are not sure if your abstraction manages complexity or not. Your abstraction *does* manage complexity if it: – gets rid of repeated code. – helps you manage the behaviors for parts of your program. – controls an important piece of your program. You should either redesign or enhance your code to make this happen.	What do you still need to do to make your program match your idea about your program? If you involve someone else, you may get more ideas. Write these ideas down in your journal. As always, capture the design changes with enough detail that you can write about them later.
6	Record your program running with a significant feature that you added. You are ready to complete your written response if: – you have had two difficulties, two opportunities, or a difficulty and an opportunity. – you have coded a significant algorithm. – you have managed complexity in a meaningful way with an abstraction.	You are missing a major feature that was in your design. To solve this, you need to decide if this feature is worth the time. – Do you need this feature as your abstraction or algorithm? – Is it important to your vision?	What do you need to do to be ready to complete your written response?

V. SELF-ASSESSMENT

You will know that you are ready to begin working on your video and your written response when you can respond "yes" to each of the following questions. These are the questions that graders will ask themselves when they read your response to decide if you should earn full credit.

Prompt in task	Question	Yes	No
1, 2a	1. Does at least one significant feature run in your program?		
All	2. Do you have a journal that captures what happened when you were designing, writing, and testing your program?		

2b	3. Do you have one of the following in two different parts of your code:
	
	  ▸ a difficulty and an opportunity?
	  ▸ two opportunities? OR
	  ▸ two difficulties?		

2b	4. Can you explain one of these:
	
	  ▸ a difficulty and an opportunity?
	  ▸ two opportunities? OR
	  ▸ two difficulties?
	
	For whichever of these three choices you choose, can you explain what it meant to your program and how the solution helped your program?		

2b	5. Can you explain your difficulty and opportunity, the two opportunities, or two difficulties so that each of the following questions is answered:
	
	  ▸ How were they part of your development process?
	  ▸ How were they resolved?		

Prompt in task	Question	Yes	No
2c	6. Think of the algorithm you wrote and plan to highlight. Then answer these questions about that algorithm: ▸ Was the algorithm developed by you? ▸ Does the algorithm integrate two or more commonly used or new algorithms? ▸ Does the algorithm use math (random numbers, inequalities, formulas, or reasoning) and logic (sequence, selection, iteration)? ▸ Can you explain the purpose of the algorithm and how this algorithm is important to the program? ▸ Can you explain how two or more of the algorithms within this algorithm function independently and also how these algorithms "fit" into the larger algorithm?		

2d	7. Think of the abstraction you wrote and plan to highlight. Then answer these questions about that abstraction:
	
	▸ Was the abstraction developed by you?
	
	▸ Does the abstraction use math (random numbers, inequalities, formulas, or reasoning) and logic?
	
	▸ Does the abstraction manage complexity?
	
	▸ Can you explain how this abstraction manages complexity?
	
	▸ Can you show in one of the following ways why this is important to the program?
	
	  – Explain what the abstraction does.
	
	  – Explain what the program would not do if the abstraction were not there.		

Using a Video to Introduce Your Program

I. OVERVIEW

A. When you submit the Create Performance Task to the College Board via the Digital Portfolio, you will upload the following three items.

1. A video of your program running a significant feature that you coded;

2. A PDF of your response to written prompts 2a through 2d;

3. A PDF of your entire program code.

B. This chapter focuses on the creation of your video to highlight a significant *feature* of your program.

II. RECOMMENDATIONS FOR THE VIDEO

A. This video is your chance to show the purpose of your program. It is required that you submit a video showing a *feature* of your program.

It should take you 30 minutes to 1 hour to complete your video for the Create Performance Task.

B. Keep in mind these guidelines when you are ready to record your video:

1. This video is what graders will view first for your Create Performance Task.

    i. Make it professional.

    ▸ Use screen capture software such as Screencast-O-Matic (*screencast-o-matic.com*), or equivalent, to record your program running on a typical computer.

    ▸ If your program is running on a smartphone, use screen capture software that is on your phone, or software that can be found as a free download.

    ▸ If you must record your program on your phone (if your program is used to make a robot move within a mobile environment, for example), use a stabilizer to prevent the image from shaking, and be sure to record in landscape mode.

    ii. Use images that are school-appropriate.

    iii. Use grammar and word choices that do not detract from your program.

    iv. The video must be unbroken.

    ▸ It can be edited for size.

    ▸ The beginning and/or end of the video can be removed if needed.

    ▸ It cannot be spliced together in separate pieces.

2. Your video cannot exceed 1 minute in length or 30 MB in size. The following tools may be helpful:

    i. Control the resolution of the video before you record. By default, screen recorders may use a resolution that is higher than you need.

    ii. Use video editing software such as WeVideo (*WeVideo.com*) to shorten the video or save it using a smaller format.

    iii. Use video compression software such as Clipchamp (*Clipchamp.com*) to decrease the resolution of the video after it has been recorded.

    iv. If your program does not run in a visual way (for example, your program causes music to play), use another tool to make the video more effective. Examples of helpful tools in this case are:

       ▸ Animoto (*animoto.com*) turns still images into a video. You can also add text and music.

       ▸ You could create a presentation using the software Prezi (*prezi.com*) that runs automatically to explain the purpose or function with words and images.

    v. If you need to edit sound files, Audacity (*audacityteam.org*) or another sound editor will help you to modify the sound.

3. The video should identify all of the following:

    i. the purpose of the program.

    ii. a feature that is important and connected to this purpose.

    iii. the language you used.

4. Your program should be running in the video.

    i. You should not show the code unless it is necessary in the development environment you are using.

    ii. The point of the video is to show a part of your program that works.

Test Tip

This video is the first thing that you will need to submit to the College Board for your Create Performance Task. Now is a great time to revisit your Digital Portfolio located at digitalportfolio.collegeboard.org. Notice that the video can be uploaded to the site under the Create Performance Task. Notice also that there are downloadable templates for the write-up of the Create Performance Task. Go ahead and download these templates. You will need them when you write your responses to the prompts.

III. **HOW TO EXPLAIN THE PURPOSE OF YOUR PROGRAM IN YOUR VIDEO**

A. To explain the purpose of your program in your video, you must narrate your video. You must include the following information in your narration:

1. The programming language you used for your Create Performance Task.

2. The purpose of the program you wrote for your Create Performance Task.

3. What feature is being illustrated in the video.

B. Here are some ideas for how to create your audible narration:

1. Approach 1: The easiest way to do this is to record your video with a microphone.

   i. Most recording software applications have the microphone as an option that you can turn on or off.

   ii. Practice what you are going to say first.

   iii. Turn the microphone on and speak clearly into it.

2. Approach 2: This approach is useful if you do not feel comfortable speaking into a microphone, or if the background noise where you are trying to record is so loud that you cannot hear your narration.

   i. Write down what you want to say and use an online Text to Speech converter such as NaturalReaders (*naturalreaders.com*).

      ▸ Be sure your narration can be read in under one minute.

      ▸ You can use Audacity or another sound recording software to record the speech audio, or you can download the sound file.

ii. Open your video in your preferred video editing software.

iii. Add the recording as audio.

C. Now, take the time to show this video to someone else. After they have viewed it, ask yourself the questions listed below. If you don't answer "Yes" to any of the questions here, take the time to remake your video so you will make a great first impression.

1. Do they understand the purpose of your program?

2. Did they hear the programming language being identified?

3. Did they understand the feature that your video is illustrating?

4. Is it clear how this feature is connected to the purpose of the program?

5. Was your video cleanly recorded, and are you pleased to know that this is the first thing your grader will see?

Congratulations on completing your video! The next four chapters of this *Crash Course* (Chapters 11–14) will focus on your written responses to prompts.

Although you need to submit your program code for your Create Performance Task, your score for this performance task depends mostly on your written responses to the prompts about your contributions to that code.

Written Response to Prompt 2a: Introducing Your Program

 OVERVIEW

A. When you submit your Create Performance Task to the College Board via the Digital Portfolio, you will upload the following three items:

1. a video of your program running a significant feature that you coded (see Chapter 10)

2. a PDF of your written responses to Prompts 2a through 2d

3. a PDF of your entire program code

B. This chapter will focus on your written response to Prompt 2a in which you explain the purpose of your program. You will find discussions of the remaining Prompts 2b, 2c, and 2d in Chapters 12, 13, and 14.

II. **TIPS FOR WRITING RESPONSES TO PROMPTS 2a–2d**

A. Here are some tips that will save you time when writing your responses to any of the prompts in the Create Performance Task:

1. Keep your program as the focus for all prompts.

2. Use the template available from the College Board Digital Portfolio.

   i. You can find this at *digitalportfolio.collegeboard.org* under the Create Performance Task.

   ii. This template counts words for you.

3. Be sure that your written response does not exceed 750 words in total for all four Prompts 2a–2d. Be sure to stay below the suggested word count for each prompt.

4. Remember that the program code is not included in the word count.

5. Refer to the following often as you write:

   i. The rubrics for the Create Performance Task

   ii. The writing prompts for the Create Performance Task

   iii. Your journal notes

III. PROMPT 2a (PURPOSE OF PROGRAM)

A. Here are some scoring guidelines to keep in mind as you write your response to Prompt 2a:

1. To earn credit for this prompt you need to have created a video of a working feature of your program.

2. This feature should be connected to the purpose of your program.

IV. KEY ASPECTS OF PROMPT 2a (EXPLAINING YOUR PURPOSE)

A. In Prompt 2a, you have approximately 150 words to:

1. identify the programming language.

2. identify the purpose of your program.

3. explain what the video illustrates.

Allow 30 minutes to 1 hour for completing your written response to Prompt 2a. Remember, if you already explained the purpose of your program and the feature in the audio that accompanies your video, you can skip Prompt 2a.

B. To maximize your credit for Prompt 2a, do the following:

1. If you have not already done so, download and open the template that makes the most sense for your computer's word processor. (You will find this template in the College Board Digital Portfolio at *digitalportfolio.collegeboard.org* under the Create Performance Task.) This template is where you will enter your response to Prompt 2a.

2. Start by answering the first two parts of Prompt 2a as briefly and clearly as you can, in about two sentences total for both parts.

   i.   Name the programming language.

   ii. Identify the purpose of your program by answering **one** of these questions about your program in your response:

   ▸ Were you trying to solve a problem?

   ▸ Were you trying to study something?

   ▸ Were you trying to create something?

Test Tip

In each of your written responses 2a–2d, include the language of the Create Performance Task Prompt to help your reader find your response and understand your intent. For Prompt 2a, for example, begin the answer to these questions with: "The purpose of my program is to . . ." Then state specifically what problem you solved, what object you were studying, or what you were trying to create.

3. After you have responded to the first two parts of Prompt 2a, you are ready to respond to the third and final part of the prompt, in which you explain the feature that your video illustrates. Devote most of your words and time to answering these two questions in your response:

   i.   Which feature does your video highlight?

   ii. How is this feature related to the purpose of your program?

Written Response to Prompt 2b: Your Development Process

Explaining your development process for Prompt 2b should take about 1 hour.

I. OVERVIEW

A. Prompt 2b asks you to write a response explaining your development process in 200 words or less. To get full credit for this prompt, you need to:

1. describe the incremental and iterative development process of your program, focusing on two distinct points in that process. You must have done one of these points independently. The second could have happened while working with someone else. These two points can be:

    i. two opportunities, OR

    ii. two difficulties, OR

    iii. one opportunity and one difficulty.

2. clearly indicate:

    i. when the difficulty or opportunity happened.

    ii. how the difficulty or opportunity helped you to meet the purpose of your program.

    iii. how the difficulty was resolved or how the opportunity led to a program improvement.

    iv. whether the development described was collaborative or independent (at least one needs to be independent).

> A difficulty or opportunity *that leads to a development (change) in your code should always be related back to the purpose of the program. In order for something to be a development, it needs to help you to accomplish the purpose of the program. It should be connected to your idea about what this program will do.*

II. HOW TO MAXIMIZE YOUR SCORE WHILE EXPLAINING YOUR PROCESS

A. To maximize your score on Prompt 2b, follow these steps:

1. If you have not already done so, download and open the template that makes the most sense for your computer's word processor. (You will find this template in the College Board Digital Portfolio at *digitalportfolio.collegeboard.org* under the Create Performance Task.) This template is where you will type your response to Prompt 2b.

2. Know the difference between incremental and iterative development processes.

    i. An *incremental* change is based on design. It tends to be a larger change.

    ii. An *iterative* change is based on figuring out how to make the code better, have more functionality, or be more organized. It tends to be a smaller change.

3. Describe or outline the steps you used to create the entire program.

    i. Use your journal to remind yourself of the key steps. These are the steps where you created something (an opportunity) or learned something (a possible difficulty) that helped make a working product.

    ii. Be sure your reader can understand how you moved from your idea to the final code and program you are handing in at the end of the task.

4. State one difficulty or opportunity that happened near the start of your program.

    i. Include the words "near the start of my program" to specify where in the development process you were coding.

    ii. Include the words "I" or "me" to indicate that your work was done independently, or include the words "we" or "my partner and I" to indicate collaboration.

       ▸ Remember that one of the two developments you write about needs to have been completed independently.

    iii. It is likely that, since you are near the start of your program, this change was incremental. Verify that this is true.

    iv. Connect the difficulty or opportunity to your program's purpose.

       ▸ Often, opportunities cause iterative changes. An example would be noticing repeated code and, instead of repeating the code, you use one procedure to handle this repeated code, and call that procedure in multiple places.

    v. To get full credit for this opportunity, do the following:

       ▸ Explain that you did not change design, so the opportunity change is iterative.

       ▸ Show how you used this opportunity by doing the following:

          – Explain that this repeated code is used often in your program and is connected to the purpose of your program.

- Describe the connection between the opportunity and the purpose of your program.

vi. Often, difficulties cause incremental changes. For example: you realize that an important algorithm you designed for your program is not working. Use paper and pencil to rethink this design. Modify the design, and then fix the code.

vii. To get full credit for this difficulty:

▸ Explain that you are changing design, so the change is incremental.

▸ Show how you used this difficulty by explaining:

- that this algorithm is important for your program to function.

- how fixing this helped meet your program's purpose.

5. State one difficulty or opportunity that happened near the middle or end of your program.

i. Include the words "near the middle" or "near the end" to specify where in the development process you were coding.

ii. Include the words "I" or "me" to indicate that your work was done independently or include the words "we" or "my partner and I" to indicate collaboration. Remember that you need at least one independent development.

iii. Since you are near the end of your program, it is likely that this change was iterative. Verify that this is true.

iv. Connect the difficulty or opportunity to your program's purpose.

v. To get full credit for any difficulty or opportunity

▸ explain that you did not change design, so the change is iterative.

> ▸ do the following to show how you used this difficulty/opportunity to improve your code:
>
>   – explain that this repeated code is used often in your program and is connected to the purpose of your program.
>
>   – describe the connection between the difficulty/opportunity and the purpose of your program.

vi. To get full credit for any difficulty/opportunity, do the following:

> ▸ explain that you are changing design, so the change is incremental.
>
> ▸ show how you used this difficulty/opportunity to improve your code by explaining:
>
>   – that this algorithm is important for your program to function.
>
>   – how fixing this helped you meet your program's purpose.

III. FINAL CHECK

When you read your final written response to Prompt 2b, be sure you are able to answer "yes" to each of the following questions. If not, revise your response to maximize your score. These are the questions that graders will ask themselves when they read your response to decide if you should earn full credit for your response.

Question	Yes	No
1. Did you provide a description or outline of the key steps you used to create your program?		
2. Did you provide two developments (difficulties or opportunities)?		
3. Did you specify if the changes were incremental or iterative?		

(continued)

Question	Yes	No
4. Did you provide examples of both incremental and iterative developments in your written explanation?		
5. Was at least one of these developments completed independently? (Did you use the words "I" and "me" to describe this development?)		
6. Did you explain how each of these developments was resolved?		
7. Did you explain how resolving these developments was related to the purpose of your program?		

Written Response to Prompt 2c: Showing and Explaining an Algorithm

Allow about 1 hour to show and explain an algorithm that you coded to respond to Prompt 2c.

I. OVERVIEW

A. Prompt 2c asks you to show and explain an algorithm that you coded to accomplish a portion of your Create Performance Task. You have 200 words to write this response.

The focus of this prompt is an algorithm that you wrote that was important for your program. The algorithm should be related to a key feature and connected to the program's purpose. Think about your intended goal or the main objective of your program, then be sure the algorithm you choose is related to accomplishing this.

B. To get full credit for this prompt, do the following:

1. Choose an algorithm that is important to your program's purpose.

2. Capture and paste the code segment that implements the algorithm.

3. Verify that the algorithm you choose satisfies all of the following requirements:

    i. The algorithm is connected to the purpose of your program.

    ii. You are the person who wrote this algorithm.

    iii. This algorithm calls at least two other algorithms.

    iv. The algorithm is complex enough to make it a good candidate for this prompt. This means that in order to create it, you needed to use at least one of the following:

    ▸ Sequencing: you needed sequencing if the order of your lines of code made a difference in the way it functioned.

    ▸ Selection: you needed selection if a decision needed to be made before continuing on in the program. You might use selection to control values to prevent errors or to add more complexity to your program. Selection statements usually involve the word "if."

    ▸ Iteration: your code required iteration if you needed to do something repeatedly. It might have been that you needed to access all elements in a collection or a list or that you needed to repeat behavior until a number was reached or a condition was satisfied.

    v. Explain each of the following key points about the algorithm:

    ▸ what this algorithm does

    ▸ why another part of the code would call it

    ▸ the key parts of this algorithm

    ▸ how this algorithm is connected to the main purpose of the program

    ▸ how one of the included algorithms functions independently

According to the latest AP scoring guidelines released, algorithms are defined as "precise sequences of instructions for processes that can be executed by a computer and are implemented using programming languages." Read this carefully. You should choose a complex algorithm to write about for this prompt.

II. HOW TO MAXIMIZE YOUR SCORE WHILE EXPLAINING YOUR ALGORITHM

A. To maximize your score on Prompt 2c, follow these steps:

1. Choose the algorithm that you plan to highlight in this prompt.

   i. The algorithm needs to meet *all* of the following requirements to be considered:

   ▸ You need to be the person who wrote the code for this algorithm.

   ▸ It must be important to your program. Proof of this would be:

   – It needs to be called by another part of your program.

   – It must call at least two other algorithms that include math or logic. (These algorithms could be for loops or *if* statements and they do not need to be written by you.)

   ▸ It should do one of the following:

   – Integrate math (random numbers, inequalities, formulas, reasoning).

   – Show you can use logic (sequencing, selection, and iteration) in your code.

ii. If you have not created an algorithm that meets these requirements:

  ▸ Look at your code for ideas so you can reorganize or enhance your code.

  ▸ Ask others to look at your code and share their ideas.

  ▸ Consider implementing more functionality into your program.

2. Prepare your algorithm to be highlighted. Be sure to do the following so you get full credit for your algorithm:

  i. Use your preferred snipping tool to make an image of your algorithm.

   ▸ Include the two algorithms that your main algorithm calls.

   ▸ Add the algorithm(s) that call(s) your algorithm, if it/they add(s) clarity.

  ii. Open your Create Performance Task template. Follow directions to copy and paste your code into the template under prompt 2c.

To help explain your algorithm, name your algorithm and the variables that it calls so that they are related to the program. For example, suppose you have a variable that is a timer. If your language allows, instead of calling it "x," call it "timer." If your language only allows single letters, call it "t."

When answering a written prompt, maximize your score by making it easy for your grader to find your response to each prompt. For example, when answering the question: "What does each algorithm called by your algorithm do alone?", start your response with: "The first algorithm called by my algorithm is a for loop. The loop does (something related to your program)." Your grader will know that these words relate to the first attribute that they are looking for in your response.

3. Draft your written response to Prompt 2c. To maximize credit earned, be sure to answer each of the following questions:

    i.   What does each algorithm called by your algorithm do alone?

    ii.   What do the algorithms called by your algorithm do together?

    iii. How does your algorithm connect to the purpose of your program?

    iv. What mathematical concepts does your algorithm use?

    v.   Where does your algorithm use logical concepts?

Test Tip

Your written explanation of your algorithm needs to do more than explain what the algorithm does; you need to explain how *the algorithm does it. These explanations should not be line-by-line explanations of your code. Instead, explain the key parts of your algorithm and how these key parts are related to each other and to the overall purpose of the program.*

III. FINAL CHECK

When you read your final written response to Prompt 2c, be sure you are able to answer "yes" to each of the following questions. If not, revise your response to maximize your score. These are the questions that graders will ask themselves when they read your response to decide if you should earn full credit for your response.

Question	Yes	No
1. Does your selected algorithm integrate two or more commonly used or new algorithms?		
2. Did you include your code segment in the written responses section? (Be sure to include the main algorithm, as well as any other algorithms called by the main algorithm that were not included with the programming language.)		
3. Does your selected algorithm integrate mathematical and/or logical concepts?		
4. Do you identify the algorithm's purpose in the program?		
5. Do you explain how the algorithm achieves this purpose?		
6. Does your response explain how at least two of the algorithms work independently?		
7. Does your response explain how at least two of the algorithms work together to create a new algorithm?		

Written Response to Prompt 2d: Showing and Explaining Your Abstraction

I. OVERVIEW

A. Prompt 2d asks you to show and explain an abstraction that you used in your code to accomplish your Create Performance Task. You have 200 words to write this response.

B. To get full credit for this prompt, do the following:

1. Capture and paste each code segment that implements the abstraction that is important to your program's function.

2. Choose an abstraction that satisfies *all* of the following requirements:

   i. The abstraction integrates mathematical and logical concepts.

   ii. The abstraction helps manage the complexity of your program.

   iii. The abstraction is connected to the purpose of the program.

It should take you about 1 hour to show and explain an abstraction that you used in your code in order to answer Prompt 2d.

II. HOW TO MAXIMIZE YOUR SCORE WHILE EXPLAINING YOUR ABSTRACTION

A. To maximize your score on Prompt 2d, follow these steps:

1. Choose the abstraction that you plan to highlight in this prompt.

   i. The abstraction needs to meet *all* of the following requirements to be considered:

      ▸ You need to be the person who wrote the code for this abstraction.

      ▸ It must be important to your program. Proof of importance would be integrating mathematical and logical concepts and/or managing complexity in your program.

      ▸ Examples of how an abstraction could manage complexity are:

         – Rather than repeating code, you use a single algorithm.

         – You wrote a large algorithm. It was hard to debug because it had so many steps. To help with debugging, you took a major piece and turned it into a procedure.

         – You used an existing abstraction to create a new abstraction. An example of this is the use of a list to represent a collection of items. If you explain how this list helps you to manage a complexity related to your program's purpose, it could fit the needs of this project.

      ▸ Examples of abstractions include:

         – Procedures

         – Parameters

- Lists
- Application Program Interfaces (APIs)
- Libraries

ii. If you have not created an abstraction that meets these requirements, do the following:

▸ Look at your code for ideas on how to reorganize or enhance your code.

▸ Consider adding functionality to the program that will facilitate the creation and use of an abstraction.

▸ If you cannot see a way to do this, have others look at your code and share their ideas.

Test Tip

Using a procedure or algorithm in your code to manage complexity is a great example of Iterative Software Design. It happens when you realize that you have repeated code that ought to be managed in one spot. This algorithm (if it calls at least two other algorithms) could be used for Prompt 2d as an abstraction. Remember to focus on how the algorithm manages complexity and connects to the purpose of the program.

2. Prepare your abstraction to be highlighted. Be sure to do the following so you get full credit for your abstraction:

i. It may help your explanations to be sure all of your variables and algorithms are named well.

ii. Make an image of your abstraction (using the snipping tool that you prefer).

iii. If the abstraction calls other algorithms or abstractions, show the code for this as well.

iv. Open your Create Performance Task Template, and follow directions to copy and paste your code into the template under Prompt 2d.

3. Draft your written response to Prompt 2d. To maximize credit earned, be sure you answer all of the following questions:

    i. How does your abstraction integrate mathematical and logical concepts?

    ii. How does your abstraction manage complexity of the program?

    iii. Does your response indicate that you developed the abstraction?

    iv. Does your response accurately explain the purpose of this abstraction within your program?

III. FINAL CHECK

When you read your final written response, be sure you are able to answer "yes" to each of the following questions. If not, revise your response to maximize your score. These are the questions that graders will ask themselves when they read your response to decide if you should earn full credit for your response.

Question	Yes	No
1. Did you develop the abstraction you are using in this prompt?		
2. Does your abstraction integrate math and logical concepts?		
3. Does your abstraction manage complexity of the program?		
4. Did you prove that this abstraction manages complexity by either (a) explaining what this abstraction does for the program, or (b) explaining what this program would not be able to do without the abstraction?		
5. Did you explain how the abstraction was developed?		

Completing Your Create Performance Task

Congratulations! If you are reading this chapter, you are almost finished with your Create Performance Task.

Allow about 2 hours to prepare your code and submit your final files to the College Board via the Digital Portfolio.

I. OVERVIEW

A. This chapter focuses on the final steps for submitting your Create Performance Task. These include:

1. preparing your code (Prompt 3).

2. preparing work to be submitted.

3. using the Digital Portfolio.

II. ORGANIZING YOUR RESPONSE TO PROMPT 3 (YOUR CODE)

A. Prompt 3 asks you to copy and paste your entire program code and share it as a PDF.

B. This is the first chance your grader will have to understand how your algorithm (Prompt 2c) and your abstraction (Prompt 2d) fit into your final program in terms of code.

C. This code can be text or it can be an image of blocks of code.

Test Tip *Show the code that you used when you were creating the program. If you used blocks, use a Snipping Tool to capture these images from your computer and show them as blocks. If you used text, copying and pasting this text is fine.*

D. This prompt does not count against your word count.

E. Any words (not code) that you type should be focused on clarifying either the code that you created or the code that was created by someone else.

   1. Here is one approach to making this clear in your final submission:

      i. Open up a document file.

      ii. Create two separate pages in that file.

      iii. Title page 1: "My Code."

      iv. Title page 2: "Code Created by Someone Else."

      v. Copy and paste code on each page. If you need multiple pages for either, include the label that makes sense on the top of each new page.

   2. If your code is too interconnected to use the above approach, then use comments in your language to clarify the work you did and then acknowledge the source of the work created by someone else.

F. Use your response to this prompt to cite any images or sound files used in your program.

G. To get full credit for Prompt 3, do the following:

   1. Mark the algorithm you wrote about in Prompt 2c with an oval.

   2. Mark the abstraction you wrote about in Prompt 2d with a rectangle.

3. Include comments or citations for program code written by someone else.

> *Remember, there are no word or page count limits for this section. Take advantage of this and make a clear presentation. Be organized and include white space when presenting your code.*

III. SUBMITTING FILES TO THE COLLEGE BOARD

A. When completing your Create Performance Task, there are three pieces of work you will need to submit to the College Board.

1. A video of a significant feature in your program

2. A PDF of your written response to Prompts 2a–2d

3. A PDF of your entire program code

IV. IMPORTANT DETAILS ABOUT YOUR VIDEO

1. The video must satisfy all of the following requirements:

   i.   The video needs to be less than 1 minute and under 30 MB;

   ii. The video should be saved with one of the following file extensions: .mp4, .wmv, .avi, or .mov.

   ▸ To find the file extension, look at the properties of the file.

   ▸ You may need to use your video editor to convert the file to an appropriate file type. If this is not possible, there are online tools that you can use to convert your file.

V. IMPORTANT DETAILS ABOUT YOUR WRITTEN RESPONSES

1. You need to upload your written responses to 2a–2d as a PDF.

2. To create this PDF, use the College Board template so that Prompts 2a–2d are shown, and your responses appear below each prompt.

3. Convert the document to a PDF by choosing to print to a PDF maker, or use an online converter. You can also make the conversion using Google Docs if you have access to the Google Docs application on your computer. To convert your document to PDF using Google Docs, follow these steps:

    i. Upload your file to Google Docs.

    ii. Choose "Download As" from the File dropdown menu.

    iii. Download the file as a PDF.

VI. IMPORTANT DETAILS ABOUT THE PROGRAM CODE

1. Be sure to do the following with your program code:

    i. Mark the algorithm you wrote about in Prompt 2c with an oval.

    ii. Mark the abstraction you wrote about in Prompt 2d with a rectangle.

    ii. Indicate which code was done by you and which code was done by someone else. Use this section to cite any image or sound files you used as well.

As a final check before you submit this task, refer to Appendix F in this book for your Create Performance Task "checklist." This checklist summarizes the key requirements based on the latest Scoring Guidelines released.

VII. USING THE DIGITAL PORTFOLIO TO SUBMIT YOUR TASK

Before you decide to press the "Final Submit" button on your Digital Portfolio, spend some time making sure you are maximizing your score. Be sure you can answer "Yes" to the following questions:

Prompt	Requirement	Yes	No
1, 2a	Does your video demonstrate the running of at least one feature of the program that is connected to the program's purpose?		
1, 2a	Does your response to 2a explicitly state the purpose of the program?		
2b	Does your response to Prompt 2b describe one of the following pairs of developments: (1) a difficulty and an opportunity, (2) two opportunities, or (3) two difficulties?		
	Was at least one of these done independently?		
2b	Does your response to Prompt 2b describe how the two developments were resolved and incorporated as part of an iterative and iterative development process?		
2c	Does the algorithm that you chose for Prompt 2c integrate two or more commonly used or new algorithms? In doing so, does it integrate math and/or logical concepts to create a new algorithm?		
2c	Does your response to Prompt 2c identify how your algorithm's purpose is connected to the program and the role that this algorithm plays in the program?		
2c	Did you describe how two of the algorithms function independently as well as together to create a new algorithm?		
2d	Does your response to Prompt 2d explain how the abstraction you chose integrates math and logical concepts?		

(continued)

Prompt	Requirement	Yes	No
2d	Does your response to 2d explain how the abstraction you chose manages complexity in the program? Did you prove this by explaining the role the abstraction plays in the purpose of the program, or by explaining how the program would be different without it?		
2d	Does your response to 2d indicate that an abstraction was developed, and did the response explain the abstraction by connecting the purpose of the abstraction to the program?		
3	Did you paste all of your code into the template and mark your algorithm with an oval, and your abstraction with a rectangle?		
3	Did you clarify the code that you wrote and identify code, if any, that was written by someone else?		
	Did you check your word counts? Be sure to keep the word count within the specified guidelines. The template provided by the College Board counts words for you.		

VIII. YOUR FINAL SUBMISSION

A. When you are ready, follow these steps to submit your work to the College Board:

1. Communicate with your school point of contact so he/she understands that you plan to submit your task.

2. Go to *digitalportfolio.collegeboard.org* and log in.

3. Find your class and click on "Create Performance Task."

4. Follow directions to upload the Video of a Feature.

   i. The site will prompt you to check the version you are uploading.

   ii. Open the file.

iii. Verify that this is the version you want to submit. Then, either submit this version or upload a different version.

5. Follow directions to upload your written responses to Prompts 2a–2d. You will be prompted to verify that this is the version you want to submit as your final version.

6. Follow directions to upload your entire program code (Prompt 3). Again, you will be prompted to verify that this is the version you want to submit as your final version.

You're done! Celebrate! You have just handed in what will become 24 percent of your AP score for AP Computer Science Principles. Take a moment to reflect on all that you've learned.

PART III

THE END-OF-COURSE EXAM

Overview of the End-of-Course Exam

I. OVERVIEW

A. As you prepare for your AP Computer Science Principles (AP CS Principles) End-of-Course Exam, keep the following details in mind:

1. The exam is administered in May during the AP exam administration window.

2. The End-of-Course Exam is 2 hours in length.

3. This part of the exam is worth 60 percent of your AP CS Principles score.

4. The End-of-Course Exam contains 74 multiple-choice questions (which allows about one-and-a-half minutes to answer each question).

5. There are two types of multiple-choice questions:

   i. Single-Select Multiple Choice

   ▸ There is one correct answer out of four possibilities (A–D).

   ▸ The majority of the multiple-choice exam questions follow this format.

   ii. Multiple-Select Multiple-Choice

   ▸ There are two correct answers out of four possibilities. You need to choose both correct answers to get credit.

6. There is no penalty for guessing.

Be sure you know when and where you will be taking the End-of-Course Exam. Check with your AP teacher for details.

II. TOPICS ON THE EXAM

A. The End-of-Course Exam will have questions on the following topics, in order of importance. Included in the chart below is the percentage of questions about that topic that you can expect to see on the exam, and the chapter in this *Crash Course* where the topic is explained.

Topic	Percentage of questions on exam	Chapter in *Crash Course* where topic is explained
Algorithms	20%	Chapter 18
Programming	20%	Chapter 19
Abstraction	19%	Chapter 20
Data and Information	18%	Chapter 21
The Internet	13%	Chapter 22
Global Impact	10%	Chapter 23

III. LANGUAGES AND INSTRUCTIONS ON THE EXAM

A. There are two types of languages you will see on the exam:

1. block

2. text

B. Programming instructions will use one of the following four data types:

1. numbers

2. Booleans

3. strings

4. lists

While studying for your AP Computer Science Principles exam, you should practice the skills you will need with the programming language of your choice. Some common programming languages are shown in Appendix B of this book. You should also become comfortable using the Exam Reference Sheet (which will be provided to you on exam day). The Exam Reference Sheet contains instructions and explanations to help you understand the format and meaning of the exam questions. The Exam Reference Sheet is reproduced in Appendix G of this book.

Practicing Programming Languages

I. PROGRAMMING LANGUAGES USED ON THE EXAM

A. As you read this chapter, keep these tips in mind:

1. The programming language you used to understand concepts may look slightly different on the AP Computer Science Principles exam. See Appendix B for common programming languages.

2. To be prepared for this exam, you should have practiced programming using one or more languages that have all of the following:

   i. A way to assign, display, and input variables.

   ii. The ability to use arithmetic operators such as addition, subtraction, multiplication, division, and modulus.

   iii. Functions (also called procedures or methods) that you can create or modify to take parameters (as inputs), perform an action, and/or return values (as outputs).

   iv. A way to compare two values as being equal or unequal (including greater than or less than).

   v. Boolean variables that can be created or used in statements to make decisions.

   vi. Conditional statements such as *if*, *else-if*, and *else*.

   vii. Iteration (loops such as a *for* loop or a *while* loop).

viii. Lists and list operations (such as how to get an item into a list or how to add or remove items from a list).

ix. A way to control how an element (such as a sprite, a pixel, a robot, or a character in a game) is moved.

II. THE EXAM REFERENCE SHEET

A. When you take your exam, you will get an Exam Reference Sheet.

1. This sheet summarizes the Programming Language you will see in the multiple-choice questions.

2. The Exam Reference Sheet was designed to give all test takers a common reference for:

   i. Two types of programming languages:

   ▸ block

   ▸ text

   ii. Ways to do the following procedures in these languages:

   ▸ perform calculations

   ▸ handle and analyze logic

   ▸ store and manipulate information in variables and lists

   ▸ evaluate the order, conditions, and looping in code

   ▸ use code to create two-dimensional movements on a screen

B. The Exam Reference Sheet is organized by the following Categories of Instruction:

1. Assignment, Display, and Input

2. Arithmetic Operators and Numeric Procedures

3. Relational and Boolean Operators

4. Selection

5. Iteration

6. List Operations

7. Procedures

8. Robot

You should be familiar with most, if not all, of these categories no matter which language or environment you chose for this course.

III. CATEGORIES OF PROGRAMMING INSTRUCTIONS

You should be prepared to handle any of the categories shown below on your exam.

Test Tip

Now is a good time to become familiar with the Exam Reference Sheet that will be provided to you when you take your exam. It is reproduced in Appendix G of this book. Refer to it as you are studying these pages. Since you will have the reference sheet when you take your exam, you do not need to memorize it.

A. Category 1: Assignment, Display, and Input

1. In computer science, there are instructions that allow you to modify (assign), see (display), or get from a user (input) in a program.

2. This is what these instructions will look like in a multiple-choice question:

How this would be used in code on the exam:	Instruction written in Text Coding Language	Instruction written in Block Coding Language
Assigns expression to a variable a.	a ← expression	a ← expression
Show the value of "expression" always followed by a space.	DISPLAY(expression)	DISPLAY expression
Accepts a value from a user and returns it.	INPUT()	INPUT

Note: The following multiple-choice questions are designed to help you practice the nuances of the code you will see in the exam. Before you try answering the questions, read through this list:

> In actual multiple-choice questions, categories are often combined to check what you know about computer science.

> The examples provided here are to help you understand the syntax of the language you will see in the exam.

> The examples here are likely easier than the questions you will see on the exam. They are here to help you become familiar with the Exam Reference Sheet and to help you practice multiple-choice questions.

Remember, this **Crash Course** *comes with a full-length practice End-of-Course Exam. When taking the practice exam, be sure to use the Exam Reference Sheet.*

EXAMPLE 1 (SNEAK PEEK):

Refer to the code shown to the right. Suppose a person wants to test this code. When they reach line 3, they type 7. What happens next?

```
Line 1: x ← 0
Line 2: DISPLAY(x)
Line 3: x ← INPUT()
Line 4: DISPLAY(x)
```

(A) An error occurs. A person cannot interact with this program using the INPUT() function. A message would print out to let the person know this.

(B) An error occurs. A person could use the INPUT() function in this way, but the assignment would not happen since nothing is returned from INPUT().

(C) The following output occurs: 0 7

(D) The following output occurs: 07

Answer: (C)

Answer choice (A) is not correct because INPUT() does exist and was called correctly as shown in the table. If Line 3 said: "INPUT() ← x", this would be an example of a syntax error since assignment happens from right to left. Answer choice (B) is not correct because INPUT() does accept and return whatever the user of the program types. Answer choice (D) is not correct because DISPLAY(expression) puts a space after printing.

Test Tip

The example questions included in this chapter will help you learn the Exam Reference Sheet. Notice that Example 1 is labeled "(Sneak Peek)." This means that Example 1 is a multiple-choice "sneak peek" question similar to what you will see on your exam. Example 2 (which shows no label) is included so you can check your understanding of the reference and/or practice code that you might see on the exam. Although it is a TRUE/FALSE question, there are no TRUE/FALSE questions on the End-of-Course Exam.

EXAMPLE 2 (TRUE OR FALSE):

The following code is equivalent to the code in Example 1.

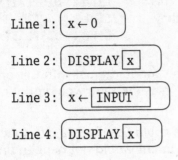

Line 1: `x ← 0`

Line 2: `DISPLAY x`

Line 3: `x ← INPUT`

Line 4: `DISPLAY x`

Answer: TRUE

Either blocks or text could be used for this exam. You need to be familiar with reading both types.

Test Tip

Notice how Example 2 refers back to the code in Example 1. It is common on the AP CS Principles exam to have groups of questions that refer back to one situation. Thus, it is in your best interest to go through the exam in order and not skip around too much. Many questions will refer back to one set of code or a specific scenario. If you skip around when answering questions, you may become confused. Reprocessing a complicated chain of questions can be a serious time sink! You can always go back to check your answers, if you have extra time after you finish.

EXAMPLE 3 (SNEAK PEEK):

A person is writing her first program. She wants the program to say "hello" to her. Here is pseudocode for what she hopes the program will do:

1. Display "Please type your name."

2. The person types her name: BELLA.

3. The computer will display: "Hello BELLA".

Which of the following programs will behave as intended?

(A) x ← INPUT()
    DISPLAY("Hello")
    DISPLAY(x)
    DISPLAY("Please type your name.")

(B) DISPLAY("Please type your name.")
    x ← INPUT()
    DISPLAY("Hello")
    DISPLAY(x)

(C) DISPLAY("Hello")
    x ← INPUT()
    DISPLAY(x)
    DISPLAY("Please type your name.")

(D) x ← DISPLAY("Please type your name.")
    DISPLAY("Hello")
    DISPLAY(x)

Answer: (B)

This question is checking that you understand that order (sequence) of code matters and that the INPUT() command is needed to get user input in a program for this language. The space will print after "Hello" since this happens by default through the call to the DISPLAY instruction. Choice (A) is incorrect because the input command is called before prompting the user. Choice (C) is incorrect because "Please type your name" should be the first call to DISPLAY. Choice (D) would be a syntax error since DISPLAY does not return anything.

B. Category 2: Arithmetic Operators and Numeric Procedures

1. These are instructions that allow you to turn two inputs into one output. All of these—the two inputs and the output—are the same type.

2. An example of an operator is addition. Notice that 2 + 3 equals 5. The inputs are 2 and 3, the output is 5, and all of these are numbers.

3. This category could be seen in code in combination with any of the other categories in a multiple-choice question.

How this would be used on the exam:	Instruction in Text or Block Language	Example of what this operation does	
Perform addition on two values a and b.	a+b	a ← 3 b ← 2 DISPLAY(a+b)	a ← 3 b ← 2 DISPLAY (a+b)
		The output: 5	
Perform subtraction on two values a and b.	a−b	a ← 3 b ← 2 DISPLAY(a−b)	a ← 3 b ← 2 DISPLAY (a−b)
		The output: 1	
Perform multiplication on two values a and b.	a*b	a ← 3 b ← 2 DISPLAY(a*b)	a ← 3 b ← 2 DISPLAY (a*b)
		The output: 6	
Perform division on two values a and b.	a/b	a ← 3 b ← 2 DISPLAY(a/b)	a ← 3 b ← 2 DISPLAY (a/b)
		The output: 1.5	

How this would be used on the exam:	Instruction in Text or Block Language	Example of what this operation does	
Find the remainder (modulus) when a is divided by b.	a MOD b	a ← 17 b ← 5 DISPLAY(a MOD b)	a ← 17 b ← 5 DISPLAY (a MOD b)
		The output: 2	
Find a random number from a to b, including a and b.	Text: RANDOM(a,b) Block: RANDOM a,b	a ← 1 b ← 3 RANDOM(a,b)	a ← 1 b ← 3 RANDOM a,b
		The output: 1, 2, or 3	

Test Tip

Both text and block languages are shown in this book next to each other. On the actual exam, a question would use one language or the other, never both.

4. **Some tips about MODULUS (MOD).** Most of the operations above are not new to you. However, modulus may be a new idea. Here are some tips to help you understand this operation:

   i. The modulus of two numbers is the remainder of these two numbers being divided.

      ▸ Here are some examples of modulus in action:

      10 MOD 1 = 0 (there is no remainder since 1 divides evenly into 10)

      10 MOD 2 = 0

      10 MOD 3 = 1

10 MOD 4 = 2 (4 divides evenly into 10 twice with a remainder of 2)

10 MOD 6 = 4 (6 divides evenly into 10 once, remainder is 4)

ii. Here are some "rules" about modulus:

▸ Any modulus calculation can be understood using long division until it becomes automatic for you.

$$\begin{array}{r} 7 \\ 3\overline{)22} \\ -21 \\ \hline 1 \end{array}$$

(remainder is 1)

Example: 22 MOD 3 is the remainder of 22 divided by 3 is shown to the right.

▸ If the number to the left of MOD is a multiple of the number to the right of MOD, the result is 0:

Example: 20 MOD 4 is 0 since 20 is a multiple of 4.

▸ If the number to the left of MOD is less than the number to the right of MOD, the result is the number to the left of MOD:

Example: 4 MOD 20 is 4 since 20 is too large to go into 4. See long division to the right.

$$\begin{array}{r} 0 \\ 20\overline{)4} \\ -0 \\ \hline 4 \end{array}$$

▸ You cannot have 0 to the right of the MOD.

(remainder is 4)

Example: 20 MOD 0 does not make sense since this would be like dividing by 0.

▸ You can have 0 to the left of the MOD.

Example: 0 MOD 4 is 0 since 0 divided by any number that is not 0 is 0 with a remainder of 0.

Test Tip

Watch for division by 0 errors in MOD calculations—this can get a little confusing. 20 MOD 0 is not valid. 0 MOD 20 is 0. The 0 cannot be to the right of MOD.

iii. Modulus is often used in a program for the following purposes:

▸ To determine if numbers are even or odd.

– If 2 is to the right of MOD, the result of this operation will tell you if the number to the left of MOD is even or odd.

Example 1: 7 MOD 2 is 1. This means 7 is odd.

Example 2: 8 MOD 2 is 0. This means 8 is even.

– General Rule:

If x MOD 2 is 1, x is ODD.

If x MOD 2 is 0, x is EVEN.

▸ To convert between number systems.

– Suppose you want to convert 1600 hours (military time) to our normal AM/PM clock time. 1600 hours is 16:00. The "normal" clock time is a 12–hour system. Applying a modulus of 12 will do the trick!

16 MOD 12 is 4. 16:00 in military time is 4:00.

– If you research *MODULUS* online, you might see it referred to as "clock time" for this reason.

EXAMPLE:

What would be displayed when each line of code (in lines 6 through 13) is reached?

```
Line 1: w ← 0
Line 2: x ← 4
Line 3: y ← 5
Line 4: z ← 0
Line 5: w ← x*y
Line 6: DISPLAY(z-x*y)
Line 7: DISPLAY(z-w)
Line 8: DISPLAY(y/x)
Line 9: DISPLAY(y MOD x)
Line 10: DISPLAY(x MOD y)
Line 11: DISPLAY(w MOD x)
Line 12: DISPLAY(z MOD x)
Line 13: DISPLAY(x MOD z)
```

Answers:

Line 6: -20 The order of operations is followed.

Line 7: -20 Since *w* was assigned *x*y*, Lines 6 and 7 are logically equivalent.

Line 8: 1.25 Division is performed.

Line 9: 1 The remainder of 5/4 is 1 since 4 goes into 5 with a remainder of 1.

Line 10: 4 The remainder of 4/5 is 4 since 5 does not go into 4. In general, since these are positive numbers and since the number to the left of MOD is smaller than the number to the right, the result is the number to the left of the MOD. So for example, 4 MOD 6 is 4, 2 MOD 7 is 2, 8 MOD 10 is 8.

Line 11: 0 The remainder of 20/4 is 0 since the result of the division is 5 with no remainder.

Line 12: 0 See explanation for Line 10 and Line 11—this is an example of both.

Line 13: This is an error. 0 to the right of MOD is invalid since you cannot divide by 0.

C. Category 3: Relational and Boolean Operators

1. A Boolean is a special data type that has one of two values: true or false.

2. A Boolean may be returned

   i.   as a result of evaluating a condition,

   ii.   as a result of comparing two values, or

   iii. when evaluating one or more Boolean conditions.

3. This category could be seen in code in combination with any of the other categories in a multiple-choice question.

How this would be used on the exam:	Instruction in Text or Block Language	Example of what this operation does	
Compares values stored in a and b. Returns true if the statement is true; false otherwise.	a = b a ≠ b a > b a < b a ≥ b a ≤ b	a ← 3 b ← 2 DISPLAY(a>b)	a ← 3 b ← 3 DISPLAY a > b
		The output: true	
Evaluates to true if condition is false; otherwise evaluates to true. You can look at NOT as the instruction that changes true to false and false to true.	Text: NOT condition Block: NOT condition	a ← 3 b ← NOT(a=3) DISPLAY(b)	a ← 3 b ← NOT a = 3 DISPLAY b
		The output: false	
Evaluates to true if condition1 <u>and</u> condition2 are true; otherwise evaluates to false.	Text: condition1 AND condition2 Block: condition1 AND condition2	a ← false b ← true c ← a AND b DISPLAY(c)	a ← false b ← true c ← a AND b DISPLAY c
		The output: false	
Evaluates to true if condition1 <u>or</u> condition2 are true; otherwise evaluates to false.	Text: condition1 OR condition2 Block: condition1 OR condition2	a ← true b ← false c ← a OR b DISPLAY(c)	a ← true b ← false c ← a OR b DISPLAY c
		The output: true	

4. Tips (and vocabulary) about Boolean operators.

   i. Applying NOT to conditions.

     ▸ When applying NOT to relational operators, be careful. The opposite of an inequality can be misleading. Specifically, see the following list:

        – NOT(a<b) is a≥b.

        – NOT(a>b) is a≤b.

        – NOT(a=b) is a≠b.

        – NOT(a≠b) is a=b.

        – NOT(a≥b) is a<b.

        – NOT(a≤b) is a>b.

     ▸ When applying NOT to statements with AND or OR, the following rules can be used. These are commonly called DeMorgan's Laws.

        – NOT (a AND b) is <u>NOT a OR NOT b</u>

        – NOT (a OR b) is <u>NOT a AND NOT b</u>

        – Even though you do not need to know these laws by name, you do need to know how to apply them to conditions in code.

EXAMPLE 1 (SNEAK PEEK):

A parking garage has two floors. To help drivers find available parking spaces, a program is used to show which floor has more spaces available for parking. Upon entering the garage, drivers see a sign with lights showing the floor numbers. If a light is on next to the floor number, parking spaces are available on that floor. If no lights are on, there are no parking spaces available on either floor. If two lights are on, both floors have available spaces. There could be 0, 1, or 2 lights on at any time.

- Each floor has the same number of spaces, stored in integer variable numSpaces.

- The program uses sensors to track if a space is free or not. These sensors are used to assign values to the last two variables (spacesFloor1 and spacesFloor2) listed in the table below.

Variable	Description
numSpaces	this integer constant holds the number of spaces possible on each floor
spacesFloor1	this integer variable holds the number of spaces available on the first floor
spacesFloor2	this integer variable holds the number of spaces available on the second floor

Using the above information only, which of the following would mean both lights are turned on?

(A) (spacesFloor1 = spacesFloor2) AND (spacesFloor1>0)

(B) (spacesFloor1 = spacesFloor2) AND (spacesFloor1=numSpaces)

(C) (spacesFloor1 = spacesFloor2)

(D) (spacesFloor1 = spacesFloor2) or (spacesFloor1>0)

Answer: (A)

Choice (A)'s statement would be true if both floors had at least one space. Choice (B)'s statement would be true if both floors were empty. Both lights would be on if spaces are available on both floors. Choice (A) is the only solution that guarantees this. Choice (B) does not guarantee both lights are on since if numSpaces were 0, no lights would be on. Choice (C) is similar to (B). Again this could be true when both floors are full. Similarly, due to the "or," choice (D) could be true when both floors are full.

EXAMPLE 2 (SNEAK PEEK):

Using the information from Example 1, which of the following would *not* mean both lights are turned off?

    (A) NOT((spacesFloor1 ≠ 0) or (spacesFloor2 ≠ 0))

    (B) (spacesFloor2 = 0) and (spacesFloor1 = spacesFloor2)

    (C) (spacesFloor1 = 0) or (spacesFloor1 = spacesFloor2)

    (D) (spacesFloor1 ≤ 0) and (spacesFloor2 ≥ 0)

Answer: (A)

Both lights would be off if both spacesFloor1 and spacesFloor2 are 0. The challenge involved in selecting choice (A) is to see that, using DeMorgan's Laws, NOT((spacesFloor1 ≠ 0) or (spacesFloor2 ≠ 0)) is NOT(spacesFloor1 ≠ 0) and NOT(spacesFloor2 ≠ 0), which is equivalent to (spacesFloor1=0) and (spacesFloor2=0). Choice (B) returns true only if spacesFloor2 is 0 and spacesFloor1 is equal (so also 0). Choice (C) would not mean both lights are turned off since this could be true when both floors have an equal number of spaces. Choice (D) returns true when spacesFloor2 ≤ 0 and spacesFloor1 ≥ 0 have point(s) in common. This is only where spacesFloor2 is 0 and spacesFloor1 is 0.

Test Tip

Remember that since Example 1 and Example 2 have "(Sneak Peek)" written next to them, they are meant to give you an idea of the type of question you should be able to handle on the End-of-Course Exam. Be sure to check out the sample AP CS Principles End-of-Course Practice Exam that accompanies this Crash Course. See the inside front cover of this book for your access code.

ii.   Short-Circuiting and Logic Gates

▸ When evaluating the final value of Boolean statements being compared using AND or OR, you can save a lot of time by noticing short circuits.

▸ There are two types of short-circuiting situations you should be able to recognize:

– If the word between two conditions is OR and the first condition is true, the result will always be true.

Written generally: true OR _____ is true

Specifically: Suppose x is 5. The conditional statement, ((x=5) OR (x>5)) is true.

– If the word between two conditions is AND and the first condition is false, the result will always be false.

Written generally: false AND _____ is false

Specifically: Suppose x is 5. Then statement ((x>5) AND (x=5)) is false. In fact, since these two situations could never be true at the same time, this would be false no matter what x's initial value was.

▸ A way to practice short-circuiting is to study logic gates. In fact, this is how questions related to short-circuiting often show up on the exam. Here are some facts about logic gates:

– A logic gate is a part of a circuit.

– A logic gate has two Boolean inputs and one Boolean output.

▶ On the exam, logic gates are shown using the following abstraction. (Note that the gates AND, OR, and NOT are represented with rectangles.)

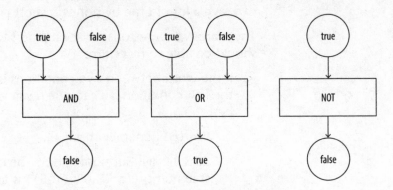

▶ Here is a Logic Table containing the possible combinations of inputs (and the output) for any logic gate.

First Input	GATE	Second Input	Output
TRUE	AND	TRUE	TRUE
TRUE	AND	FALSE	FALSE
FALSE	OR	FALSE	FALSE
FALSE	OR	TRUE	TRUE
FALSE	AND	TRUE or FALSE	FALSE
TRUE	OR	TRUE or FALSE	TRUE

▶ Notice the short-circuiting shown in the table.

a. The last two rows show short-circuiting "in action."

b. The fact that the circuit only depends on the first input is why it is called short-circuiting.

EXAMPLE 3 (SNEAK PEEK):

The figure to the right shows a circuit composed of two logic gates. The output of the circuit is true.

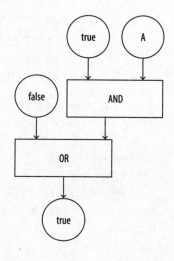

Which of the following is a true statement about input A?

(A) Input A must be false.

(B) Input A must be true.

(C) Input A could be either true or false.

(D) There is no possible value of input A that will cause the circuit to have the output true.

Answer: (B)

Look at these types of problems from the bottom up, rather than the top down. If the result of an OR gate is true this means that one of the inputs is true. The input shown is false. Therefore, the result from the AND gate must be true. The only way that an AND gate returns true is if both inputs are true. Input (A) must be true.

You could also refer to the Logic Table on the prior page, see the output, and determine the options for the input.

D. Category 4: Selection

1. Selection is one of the three major components of any algorithm in computer science. The other two components are sequencing (order) and iteration (moving through a collection).

2. In an algorithm, selection is used for the following situations:

   i. You know what you want to do when a condition is true. This is often called an IF-statement.

   ii. You know what you want to do when a condition is false. This is often the ELSE in an IF-ELSE statement.

3. This is what *selection* instructions will look like in a multiple-choice question:

How this would be used on the exam:	Instruction in Text	Instruction in Block

The code in <block of statements> would be executed only if the Boolean expression condition is true; nothing would happen if condition is false	IF(condition)
	{
	<block of statements>
	}
		IF condition
		
		block of statements

The code in <first block of statements> is executed if condition is true; otherwise the code in <second block of statements> is executed	IF(condition)
	{
	<first block of statements>
	}
	ELSE
	{
	<second block of statements>
	}
		IF condition
		
		first block of statements
		
		ELSE
		
		second block of statements

EXAMPLE 1 (SNEAK PEEK):

Consider the code segment below.

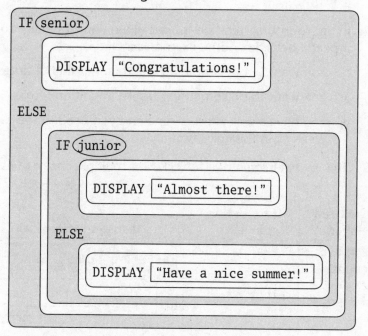

```
IF (senior)

    DISPLAY "Congratulations!"

ELSE

    IF (junior)

        DISPLAY "Almost there!"

    ELSE

        DISPLAY "Have a nice summer!"
```

If the variable *junior* is false, what is displayed?

    (A) "Have a nice summer!"

    (B) "Congratulations!"

    (C) Both A and B

    (D) It is impossible to determine.

Answer: (D)

Information about whether the Boolean variable senior is true or not is not included. If senior is true, then "Congratulations!" would display. If not, only "Have a nice summer!" would display.

E. Category 5: Iteration

    1. Iteration is one of the three major components of any algorithm in computer science. The other two components

are sequencing (order) and selection (using *if* statements or *if-else* statements to choose which block of statements will execute).

2. In an algorithm, iteration is used when you would like to repeat a behavior. Some examples include:

   i.   You want to do something a certain number of times.

   ii. You want to do something until a condition is true.

   iii. You have a collection of data and you need to see each element in the collection.

3. This is what *iteration* will look like in a multiple-choice question:

How this would be used on the exam:	Instruction in Text	Instruction in Block

The code in block of statements would be executed n times	REPEAT n TIMES
	{
	<block of statements>
	}
		REPEAT n TIMES
		  block of statements

The code in block of statements would be executed until the Boolean expression condition is true.	REPEAT UNTIL (condition)
	{
	<block of statements>
	}
		REPEAT until condition
		  block of statements

The variable item holds each element of list in order from first element to last element. The code in block of statements is executed once for each time item is assigned.	FOR EACH item in list
	{
	<block of statements>
	}
		FOR EACH item IN list
		  block of statements

EXAMPLE 1 (SNEAK PEEK):

Consider the following code segment.

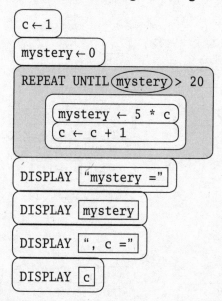

What is displayed as a result of running the program code?

(A) mystery = 20, c = 5

(B) mystery = 25, c = 6

(C) mystery = 30, c = 6

(D) mystery = 25, c = 5

Answer: (B)

Tables can help in tracing loops. Before the loop, mystery is 0 and c is 1. The loop condition is not evaluated until the last block in the loop is processed.

Loop number	mystery	c
1	5	2
2	10	3
3	15	4
4	20	5
5	25	6

EXAMPLE 2 (SNEAK PEEK):

Which of the following block of code does NOT display the same values as Example 1?

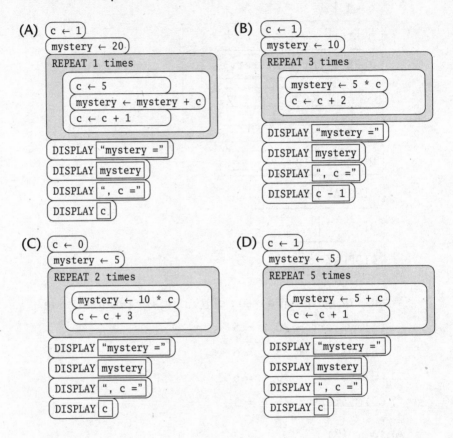

(A)
```
c ← 1
mystery ← 20
REPEAT 1 times
    c ← 5
    mystery ← mystery + c
    c ← c + 1
DISPLAY "mystery ="
DISPLAY mystery
DISPLAY ", c ="
DISPLAY c
```

(B)
```
c ← 1
mystery ← 10
REPEAT 3 times
    mystery ← 5 * c
    c ← c + 2
DISPLAY "mystery ="
DISPLAY mystery
DISPLAY ", c ="
DISPLAY c - 1
```

(C)
```
c ← 0
mystery ← 5
REPEAT 2 times
    mystery ← 10 * c
    c ← c + 3
DISPLAY "mystery ="
DISPLAY mystery
DISPLAY ", c ="
DISPLAY c
```

(D)
```
c ← 1
mystery ← 5
REPEAT 5 times
    mystery ← 5 + c
    c ← c + 1
DISPLAY "mystery ="
DISPLAY mystery
DISPLAY ", c ="
DISPLAY c
```

Answer: (D)

This block would display: mystery = 30, c = 6. All of the other blocks of code can be traced using a table to confirm that their output is the same output as Example 1.

F. Category 6: List Operations

1. A list is a collection of items of the same type.

2. Lists are handled differently in each language. It is important to know the following:

    i. The way lists are created, modified, and accessed on the Exam Reference Sheet may have a different syntax from what you practiced.

    ii. No matter the language, a common vocabulary is important:

    ▸ the list = the collection itself

    ▸ the index = the location in the list where an item can be found

    ▸ the item = one element of the list

3. Here are some key points about lists when considering the AP CS Principles End-of-Course Exam:

    i. An error is returned if you try to access an element that is outside of the list:

    ▸ The smallest list index is 1.

    ▸ The largest list index is the length of the list.

    ii. You can add elements to a list in three ways:

    ▸ You can initialize from a list of values (assignment by list variable).

    ▸ You can add one element at a time at the end of the list (called APPEND).

    ▸ You can add one element at a time at a specific location in the list (called INSERT).

    iii. You can remove elements from the list by their location (called REMOVE).

    iv. When elements are added or removed, the length of the list is automatically adjusted.

4. Details of list operations.

How this would be used on the exam:	Instruction in Text	Instruction in Block
Returns the element of list at index i.	list[i]	list i
Returns the first element of list.	list[1]	list i
Assigns the value of list[j] to list[i].	list[i] ← list[j]	list i ← list j
Assigns value1, value2, and value3 to list[1], list[2], and list[3], respectively.	list ← [value1, value2, value3]	list ← value1, value2, value3
The variable item holds each element of list in order from first element to last element. The code in block of statements is executed once for each time item is assigned.	FOR EACH item in list { <block of statements> }	FOR EACH item IN list block of statements
Inserts value into list at location i. Shifts values in locations larger than i to the right. Increases length of list by 1.	INSERT(list, i, value)	INSERT list, i, value
Place value at end of list. Increase length of list by 1.	APPEND(list, value)	APPEND list, value

How this would be used on the exam:	Instruction in Text	Instruction in Block
Remove item at index i from the list and shifts any values at locations larger than i to the left. Reduces length of list by 1.	REMOVE(list, i)	REMOVE list, i
Returns the length of the list	LENGTH(list)	LENGTH list

EXAMPLE 1 (SNEAK PEEK):

A retail company uses a database to store key statistics. The prices of all items in the store are stored in a list called priceList indexed from 1 to n. The company uses the following program to assign the *index of the item* in the store that has the highest price to the variable max.

```
i ← 0
max ← i + 1
n ← LENGTH(priceList)
REPEAT n times
{
    i ← i + 1
    <MISSING CODE>
}
```

Which of the following code segments can replace <MISSING CODE> so that the program works as intended?

(A) IF(priceList[i] > max)
```
{
    max ← priceList[i]
}
```

(B) IF(priceList[i] > priceList[max])
```
{
    max ← i
}
```

```
(C) IF(priceList[i] < priceList[max])
    {
        max ← i
    }
(D) IF(priceList[i] > priceList[max])
    {
        max ← priceList[i]
    }
```

Answer: (B)

The question wants you to assign the index, not the element itself, to max. Choice (D) assigns the element to max. Choice (A) compares the value stored at i to max, which is not a value in the list. Choice (C) uses an incorrect inequality, but does correctly pass the index.

EXAMPLE 2:

A track coach is writing code to track the mile times of runners on her team over the year. She has an alphabetized list of each team member's name called namesList. When a new team member is added to her team, she wants to add this person to the list in the correct spot. Which list operations are probably *not* a part of this solution? Select **two** answers.

(A)   APPEND

(B)   INSERT

(C)   REMOVE

(D)   LENGTH

Answers: (A), (C)

It is more likely that the name would not be appended (placed at the end) of the list. Using INSERT instead of APPEND makes sense since INSERT works for all situations, including the situation where the name would be inserted at the end of the list. A loop will be needed to find where in the list you will need to insert the new name. LENGTH is needed to be sure that your loop does not go outside the list. REMOVE removes elements of the list, which is not related to this problem.

There are two types of multiple-choice questions on the End-of-Course exam: single-select multiple-choice and multiple-select multiple-choice. Example 2 above is an example of a multiple-select multiple-choice question for which there are two correct answers. The exam lists these types of questions separately from the other types of multiple-choice questions and specifies that two answers are correct. You need to choose both correct answers in order to earn credit for the question. No partial credit is awarded.

EXAMPLE 3 (SNEAK PEEK):

Refer to the namesList from Example 2. Assume that the namesList has at least five names. The track coach wants to write code to display all of the elements in namesList.

Which of the following code segments will *NOT* function as intended?

(A)

```
FOR EACH name IN namesList
    DISPLAY name
```

(B)

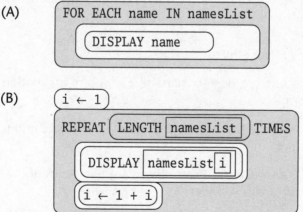

```
i ← 1
REPEAT LENGTH namesList TIMES
    DISPLAY namesList[i]
    i ← 1 + i
```

(C)

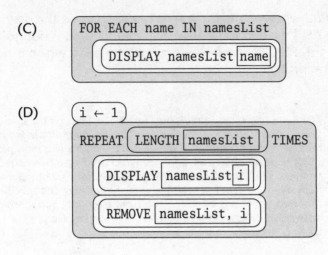

(D)

Answer: (C)

All of the other blocks display each element of the list. Choices (A) and (B) accomplish the same task, but choice (A) uses a FOR EACH loop and choice (B) uses a REPEAT loop. Notice how much easier it is to read choice (A) rather than choice (B), though they are equivalent. Choice (B) requires an extra variable not needed in choice (A). Choice (D) would be a strange approach, since the list is empty at the end of this loop, but it does display each element before removing it. Choice C does not work correctly. It would return an error since name is the name itself, not an index of namesList.

G. Category 7: Procedures

1. A procedure is a way to manage a group of instructions in a program.

2. Each language has its own unique way to create and use a procedure.

3. In the End-of-Course Exam, there are two types of procedures you will see:

   i.   a procedure that manages a group of instructions; and

   ii. a procedure that manages instructions and returns a result caused by these instructions.

4. For either type of procedure:

   i. You can have 0 or more parameters. It is possible that a procedure has no inputs (parameters).

   ii. To call the procedure without creating an error, include the name of the procedure and the correct number of parameters.

   iii. Do not worry about the data type of the parameters.

   ▸ Whether they are numbers or strings, for example, will be specified in the question.

   ▸ The question will explain their type using the name of the parameter.

5. What a PROCEDURE will look like on your exam:

How this would be used on the exam:	Instruction in Text	Instruction in Block
PROCEDURE tells the program to complete instructions. PROCEDURE can have 0 or more inputs (parameters).	PROCEDURE name(parameter1, parameter2,...) { <instructions> }	PROCEDURE name parameter1, parameter2,... instructions
PROCEDURE tells the program to complete instructions. PROCEDURE can have 0 or more inputs (parameters). This PROCEDURE is different since it returns the value of expression. The RETURN can appear anywhere in the PROCEDURE and causes a return from the PROCEDURE back to the program that called it.	PROCEDURE name(parameter1, parameter2,...) { <instructions> RETURN (expression) }	PROCEDURE name parameter1, parameter2,... instructions RETURN expression

EXAMPLE 1 (SNEAK PEEK):

A person is using a list to track the number of minutes walked each day. The list is called minutesList. It is indexed from 1 to n. Each element represents the minutes for each day. For example, minutesList[1] would return the minutes the person walked on day 1.

This person wants to write a procedure, called findAverage that calculates the average number of minutes walked per day. This procedure will take minutesList as an input and return the average as output. The code below was a first attempt, but there is an error.

What is the error?

```
PROCEDURE findAverage theList

    sum ← 0
    i ← 1

    REPEAT LENGTH theList

        sum ← theList i + sum
        i ← i + 1

    ave ← sum/LENGTH theList
    DISPLAY ave
```

(A) There is no n, so the loop will not stop.

(B) theList is different from minutesList so this procedure would not work correctly for minutesList.

(C) The following line has an error:

```
ave ← sum/LENGTH theList
```

(D) A return statement is missing.

Answer: (D)

Choice (A) is incorrect since n is equal to the return from the call to LENGTH since no elements were added or lost. Choice (B) is incorrect since this PROCEDURE would work with any list you use to call it. The call to this PROCEDURE would include minutesList as the parameter. Inside the procedure, theList is assigned minutesList. Choice (C) might have been tempting if, when you looked at this you thought, "What if theList has no elements?" This would be a reasonable error. However, since the question said that the list is indexed from 1 to n, you can assume that there is at least one element. In the question, the procedure was described as having a return instead of the DISPLAY. Therefore, Choice (D) is correct.

EXAMPLE 2 (SNEAK PEEK):

Suppose that the findAverage procedure works as described in Example 1 above. Assume that minutesList exists and you are trying to use the findAverage procedure to display the average.

Which of the following is NOT an appropriate way to call this procedure to accomplish this task? Select **two** answers.

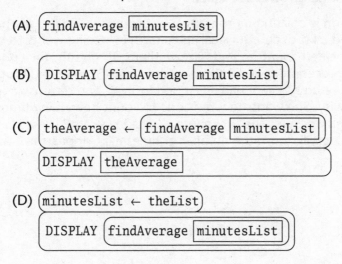

(A) findAverage minutesList

(B) DISPLAY findAverage minutesList

(C) theAverage ← findAverage minutesList
    DISPLAY theAverage

(D) minutesList ← theList
    DISPLAY findAverage minutesList

Answers: (A), (D)

Choice (A) is not appropriate since the average would be returned, but not displayed. Choice (D) is not appropriate since `theList` overrides `minutesList`. Choices (B) and (C) both correctly pass the parameter (`minutesList`) and display the output.

> *In Example 2, notice how both choices (A) and (D) are typical coding solutions to this problem. Deciding between them would be a matter of coding style, since both are clear. This question was designed to check that you noticed that you needed to display the result and that you understood how to call a procedure. In Example 1, the question has much more code to read through and one of the solutions is correct, but not elegant. The question is also more difficult because you need to read carefully about what you are required to do and go against some of what you practiced while coding to find the correct answer. (The correct answer may not be the type of code you would write!)*

EXAMPLE 3 (SNEAK PEEK):

A person is creating a program about countries. So far, she has created a list of countries called `countryList`. She wants to check for repeated countries and remove them. To do this, the code may use a procedure called `isFound(list, name)`. `isFound(list, name)` returns `true` if name is found in `list` and returns `false` otherwise. She wants to write code to count how many times a country occurs. The procedure is called `howManyTimes(list, name)`. It will return the number of times `name` appears in `list`.

Which of the following could be correct implementations of howManyTimes?

Select **two** answers.

(A)
```
PROCEDURE howManyTimes(list, name) {
    count ← 0
    REPEAT LENGTH(list) TIMES {
        IF (NOT(isFound(list, name))) {
            RETURN(0)
        }
        ELSE {
            RETURN(count)
        }
    }
}
```

(B)
```
PROCEDURE howManyTimes(list, name) {
    count ← 0
    REPEAT LENGTH(list) TIMES {
        IF (isFound(list, name)) {
            count ← count + 1
        }
    }
    RETURN (count)
}
```

(C)
```
PROCEDURE howManyTimes(list, name) {
    i ← 1
    count ← 0
    REPEAT LENGTH(list) TIMES {
        IF (isFound(list, name)) {
            count ← count + 1
            REMOVE(list, i)
        }
        ELSE {
            i ← i + 1
        }
    }
    RETURN (count)
}
```

```
(D) PROCEDURE howManyTimes(list, name) {
      i ← 1
      count ← 0
      FOR EACH item IN list {
        IF (item = name) {
          count ← count + 1
        }
        i ← i + 1
      }
      RETURN (count)
    }
```

Answers: (C), (D)

In choice (A), count is never given a value. In choice (B), if name is in list, count will be incremented each time the loop occurs since isFound will keep returning true. In choices (C) and (D), there are two different solutions. Choice (C) uses isFound and the REMOVE method to prevent adding count in each loop (unless name is found repeatedly). Choice (D) uses a FOR EACH loop and does not use isFound. While both choices (C) and (D) do return count, as described, you could describe choice (D) as a more elegant solution since (D) has less detail and is clearer. In addition, choice (C) removes elements in the list, which was not part of the algorithm described and may lead to issues elsewhere in this code. While choice (D) would be preferred, both choices (C) and (D) would be required for full credit on this question.

H. Category 8: Robot

1. This category gives you a way to move around a two-dimensional grid.

2. With these types of questions, you can count on the following:

   i. The triangle is the robot.

       ▸ The triangle points in the direction the robot is facing.

‣ The robot shown below is in the top left corner and is facing up.

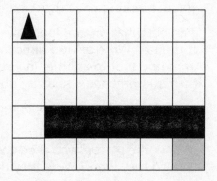

‣ The robot cannot make an "illegal" move. This means that it cannot go into the solid black squares or leave the grid.

ii. The robot may or may not be moving in toward a goal.

‣ If the robot is moving toward a goal, this would be explained in the question.

‣ In addition, the goal would be indicated with a symbol (other than the triangle) to show you where the goal is located in the grid. Often, it is a gray square as shown here.

iii. Note that some sections may be filled in.

‣ When sections of the grid are filled in, it means one of two things:

  – The robot cannot go to those parts of the grid (often filled in with black, comparable to walls in a maze).

  – The robot is trying to go to that part of the grid (filled in with gray).

‣ The question would explain what each color represents.

3. The best way to prepare for these types of questions is to do the following:

i. Practice writing code that creates visual movement.

ii. Plan out what motion looks like without using a computer. Write driving directions or steps to move from one spot to another in your neighborhood, and then ask someone else to try them out.

▸ Try to use the robot operations from the chart below.

▸ Ask the person who tried them to evaluate them: Did they work? Were they detailed enough?

▸ Consider how you might improve them. Could you use a loop or selection statements?

▸ Here are some more details about robot operations.

How this would be used on the exam:	Instruction in Text	Instruction in Block
The robot moves one square forward in the direction it is facing.	MOVE_FORWARD()	MOVE_FORWARD
The robot rotates 90 degrees counterclockwise (turns left of direction facing).	ROTATE_LEFT()	ROTATE_LEFT
The robot rotates 90 degrees clockwise (turns right of direction facing).	ROTATE_RIGHT()	ROTATE_RIGHT
Evaluates to true if there is an open square one square in the direction. Otherwise, evaluates to false. The value of direction can be left, right, backward, or forward.	CAN_MOVE(direction)	CAN_MOVE(direction)

EXAMPLE 1:

The following question uses a robot in a grid of squares. The robot is represented as a triangle, which is initially in the top left square facing up. (See accompanying grid.)

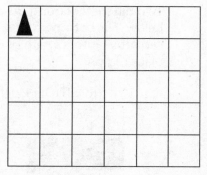

If you want the robot to end up in the bottom right square facing up, write steps/pseudocode to make this happen. Try to use ROBOT procedures as much as possible.

Answer:

There are many! Some might be more complicated than others.

In your first approach, you might have said:

> ROTATE RIGHT
>
> MOVE FORWARD x 4
>
> ROTATE RIGHT
>
> MOVE FORWARD x 4
>
> ROTATE RIGHT
>
> ROTATE RIGHT

Notice how this could be reduced to the following:

> REPEAT 2 TIMES
>
> ROTATE RIGHT
>
> REPEAT 4 TIMES
>
> MOVE FORWARD
>
> REPEAT 2 TIMES
>
> ROTATE RIGHT

Pseudocode is a bridge between requirements and actual code. Oftentimes, it follows the logical order of code, but the language is easier for humans to understand. For example, see how "x 4" is used instead of "repeat" in the first approach in Example 1 above. Pseudocode could help you to plan solutions in robot questions.

EXAMPLE 2:

Two different starting positions of a robot are shown in the grids below. For both positions, robots are initially facing up. The robot can move into a white or gray square, but cannot move into a black region.

POSITION I: POSITION II:

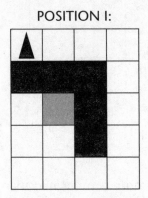
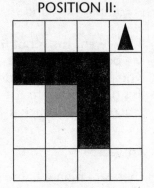

The program below was written to move the robot to the gray square. The program uses the procedure GOAL_REACHED(), which evaluates to true if the robot is in the gray square and evaluates to false otherwise.

```
REPEAT UNTIL GOAL_REACHED() {
    IF CAN_MOVE(forward) {
        REPEAT UNTIL (NOT(CAN_MOVE(forward))
            MOVE_FORWARD()
    }
    ELSE IF CAN_MOVE(right) {
        ROTATE_RIGHT()
        REPEAT UNTIL (NOT(CAN_MOVE(forward))
            MOVE_FORWARD()
    }
    ELSE {
        ROTATE_LEFT()
        REPEAT UNTIL (NOT(CAN_MOVE(forward))
            MOVE_FORWARD()
    }
}
```

In which starting position could the robot be to move correctly to the gray square?

(A) Either Position I or Position II

(B) Neither Position I nor Position II

(C) Position I only

(D) Position II only

Answer: (A)

Either Position I or Position II would work. The best way to see each of these is to place your pencil (or a small object) onto the grid and move it as the code specifies. Position II means that the loop would need to run many more times than in Position I.

IV. SUMMARY

A. The Exam Reference Sheet is a summary of the type of programming instructions that will be used on the End-of-Course Exam.

    i. The instructions will be block or text in style.

    ii. The instructions are organized into eight categories.

B. The best way to learn programming is to practice programming to solve problems on a computer.

Key Topics Related to Algorithms

I. OVERVIEW

A. About 20 percent of the End-of-Course Exam questions (15 of the 74 questions) will focus on algorithms.

B. In addition, Prompt 2c of the Create Performance Task also relates to this topic (see Chapter 13).

II. WHAT IS AN ALGORITHM?

A. An algorithm is a series of steps to execute a behavior in a program.

B. Algorithms are studied for efficiency (called *Big O notation*).

C. Algorithms are developed to understand or solve problems.

III. WHAT YOU NEED TO KNOW ABOUT ALGORITHMS

A. Algorithms are the "actions" of a program.

B. Every algorithm can be created using some or all of the following:

1. sequencing (the order that steps happen)

2. selection (conditions that control the flow of the algorithm)

3. iteration (a repeated action that is managed in a loop)

C. Given one problem, there could be more than one algorithm that could solve it.

D. Correct algorithms can be combined to make stronger code.

E. If you can write an algorithm in one language, you can write it in most other languages.

F. If you know that an algorithm works, you can use it in more than one place.

G. Breaking problems into smaller algorithms is a good way to organize your work.

H. Before deciding to use an algorithm in code, decide if it is readable and efficient.

I. Readable algorithms have the following characteristics:

1. Names of procedures and variables are related to the problem being solved.

2. Repeated code is managed using a procedure whenever possible.

3. Coding blocks are reasonable in size. To manage length, consider the following:

   i. Procedures can be created to manage repeated or important behaviors.

   ii. Objects can be created to manage actors in a program.

   iii. The vocabulary may change depending on the language you are using.

   ▸ Procedures may be called *methods* or *functions.*

   ▸ Objects might be called *sprites.*

   iv. Some languages do not allow you to create objects.

IV. THE STEPS FOR WRITING ALGORITHMS

A. Plan Code. Ways to plan code before a large project include:

1. Diagram key objects.

2. Use flowcharts to see flow of logic.

3. Use pseudocode:

    i. The term *pseudocode* is shorthand for code.

    ii. Often, pseudocode shows the steps and order.

B. Write Code (actual code).

1. You need the following to write code:

    i. A programming language

    ii. A development environment

2. Your code syntax needs to be good to be able to test code behavior.

    i. Syntax is "grammar" in an algorithm.

    ii. Your directions need to make sense in your language.

    iii. A *syntax error* means that you tried to do something that your language does not understand.

3. The development environment acts as a translator.

    i. It helps the computer understand what you wrote.

    ii. It gives you clues for how to run code.

C. Test Code (run code and check its behavior).

1. Just because code runs does not mean the code works as intended.

2. When code can be run, it has no syntax errors.

3. Code that does not run as intended is often a semantic error.

    i.   Semantic errors are caused by a mistake in logic.

    ii. Semantic errors may not be detected without testing.

V. MORE ABOUT ALGORITHMS

A. If an algorithm runs in reasonable time, it means:

1. The number of steps it takes is less than or equal to a polynomial function of the size of the input.

    i.   It is faster (takes less time) than an exponential function.

    ii. An example of an exponential function is 2^x (the variable is in the power).

    iii. An example of a polynomial function is x^2 (the variable is raised to a power).

    iv. Algorithms that require an unreasonable amount of time may solve the problem correctly, but they may not be useful because they take too long to execute.

2. The algorithm may have used a heuristic to improve its speed.

    i.   A *heuristic* is a set of rules used to get closer to a solution.

    ii. A heuristic makes sense if an approximate solution is good enough.

    iii. Heuristics can be applied to solve problems faster.

To understand the difference between an exponential and a polynomial function, and to see how x^2 is considered to run in reasonable time but 2^x is not, consider the function's behavior as x gets larger. First, you need to know that each function represents the number of comparisons, so the larger the result of each, the worse the performance. When x = 2, the difference is not clear. In fact, $x^2 = 2^x$. If, however, you increase x by 1, x = 3, and the result is also misleading. This would mean, $x^2 = 3^2 = 9$ and $2^x = 2^3 = 8$. When x = 3, 2^x is a smaller value (so less comparisons) than x^2. To see why 2^x is larger than x^2, you need to consider much larger numbers. For example, consider x = 10. $x^2 = 10^2 = 100$ and $2^x = 2^{10} = 1024$. The number of comparisons required is much more for 2^x when compared to x^2 as x increases. This would be true for any constant. In general, 3^x is much larger than x^3. If k were any number, k^x would be much larger than x^k. This is why algorithms with exponential behavior (k^x) are not considered reasonable in time.

B. Not every problem can be solved using an algorithm.

   1. Problems that cannot be solved with an algorithm are called *unsolvable*.

   2. Problems that cannot be solved in reasonable time are called *intractable*.

   3. Problems that have a "yes" or "no" answer for all inputs are called *decidable*.

   4. Problems that do not have a "yes" or "no" answer for all inputs are called *undecidable*.

      i. Some instances of undecidable problems may have a solution.

      ii. Often, these instances are limited versions of the problem.

C. Algorithms are described using mathematical patterns and denoted using Big O notation.

   1. *Big O notation* means "on the order of."

      i. It is a shortened way to describe the efficiency of an algorithm.

      ii. Efficiency of the algorithm includes both of the following:

         ▸ Memory usage of the algorithm

         ▸ Execution time of the algorithm

      iii. Efficiency is determined using mathematical reasoning about the algorithm.

      iv. Efficiency is tested by running the algorithm with different inputs.

   2. Two algorithms could correctly solve a problem and have different efficiencies.

      i. Efficient algorithms are sometimes more complex.

      ii. Since more efficient algorithms execute in less time, they may help solve larger problems.

D. Some algorithms are described by their purpose.

      i. Encryption algorithms help keep data transmission secure.

      ii. Optimization algorithms give the best solution from a list of choices.

      iii. Search algorithms find an element in a set of data.

      iv. Sorting algorithms put sets of data in order.

VI. BE ABLE TO DO THE FOLLOWING WITH ALGORITHMS:

A. Transition between words, pseudocode, and code.

    i.   Pseudocode is the bridge that connects what you want the program to do with code that the computer can understand.

    ii. Designing software means moving through these three phases (words, pseudocode, and code) in the following two ways:

        ▸ Incrementally: when a part of your design is completed, it is put into the larger project.

        ▸ Iteratively: revisiting code after completed to revise and improve a program.

Words
(Purpose)

Pseudocode
(Steps)

Code
(Program)

EXAMPLE 1 (SNEAK PEEK):

A programmer is writing code to swap two values. The procedure will follow these steps:

1. Ask the user for the first value. Store in value1.

2. Ask the user for the second value. Store in value2.

3. Swap values so what was stored in value1 is stored in value2.

4. Show that swap happened by displaying value1 and value2.

Which code correctly implements this plan?

```
(A) value1 ← INPUT()
    value2 ← INPUT()
    value2 ← value1
    value1 ← value2
    DISPLAY("value1: " + value1)
    DISPLAY("value2: " + value2)
```

```
(B) value1 ← INPUT()
    value2 ← INPUT()
    temp ← value1
    value2 ← temp
    value1 ← temp
    DISPLAY("value1: " + value1)
    DISPLAY("value2: " + value2)

(C) value1 ← INPUT()
    value2 ← INPUT()
    temp ← value1
    value1 ← value2
    value2 ← temp
    DISPLAY("value1: " + value1)
    DISPLAY("value2: " + value2)

(D) value1 ← INPUT()
    value2 ← INPUT()
    DISPLAY("value1: " + value2)
    DISPLAY("value2: " + value1)
```

Answer: (C)

For a swap algorithm to correctly swap values, you need a temporary variable. First pass one of the values to the temp, then pass the second value to the memory location of the first value. Then temp (which holds what was in the first location) is passed to the memory location of the second value.

B. Recognize and evaluate standard algorithms.

   1. Find the minimum of a list.

   i. Finding the minimum of a list involves the following key pieces:

   ▸ two data structures: a list and a variable to hold the minimum when found

   ▸ a loop to access each element in the list

ii.   The pseudocode for finding the minimum of a list is:

```
min = list[1]
for each item in list
   if item < min
      min = item
return min
```

2. Find the maximum of a list.

   i.   Involves the same key pieces as minimum (two data structures and a loop)

   ii.   The pseudocode for finding the maximum will look like the following:

```
max = list[1]
for each item in list
   if item > max
      max = item
return max
```

The key step for maximum and minimum is the if statement. The if statement could be written in the opposite direction (instead of "if item > max" it could be "if max < item.") The key is that the if statement is looking to see if there is an item in the list that could replace the initial element. Also note that the initial value of min and max is an item in the list. By using an item instead of 0, for example, we are not assuming anything about the list items. For example, 0 for min is used and there are no elements larger than 0, the min would never be set to an item in the list.

3. Find the sum of numbers.

   i.   Finding the sum of a list involves the following:

   ▸ two data structures: a list and a variable to hold the sum when calculated

   ▸ a loop to get to each item in the list

ii. Pseudocode for finding the sum might look like the following:

```
sum = 0
for each item in list
    sum = item + sum
return sum
```

4. Find the average of a set of numbers.

i. Finding the average of a list involves:

‣ three data structures: a list and two variables to hold the sum and then the average when calculated

‣ a loop to get to each item in the list

ii. To calculate the average, you need the sum. Here is possible pseudocode for average:

```
average = 0
sum = 0
for each item in list
    sum = item + sum
if (length of list) >= 1
    average = sum /(length of list)
return average
```

Note that in the algorithm for average, the **if** *statement checks that there is at least one element in the list before dividing. This prevents division by 0. If there is no element in the list, this algorithm would return 0 as the average.*

5. Search for an element (often called a "target") in a list.

i. Finding an element in a list involves:

‣ two data structures: a list and a variable to hold the location if found

‣ a loop to get to each item in the list

  ii. There are two algorithms for finding a target that you need to know:

  ▸ linear search

  ▸ binary search

The next section focuses on these two algorithms.

EXAMPLE 2 (SNEAK PEEK):

Which of the following algorithms, given a list of integers, require both selection and iteration?

  (A) An algorithm that swaps the first and last elements of the list.

  (B) An algorithm that calculates the sum of the elements in the list.

  (C) An algorithm that returns true if the first element equals the second.

  (D) An algorithm that returns the number of elements that are positive.

Answer: (D)

Choice (A) is not correct because swapping requires the creation of a third variable, not iteration. Choice (B) is incorrect because finding the sum of a list does not require selection, since the entire list will be summed. Choice (C) is incorrect because testing for equality is a conditional statement, not iteration. The only algorithm that requires both selection and iteration is choice (D), since you need to use a conditional to test if the number is positive, and iteration to access all members of the list.

VII. USING LINEAR AND BINARY SEARCHES

A. Know the difference between linear (sequential) search and binary search. (These are the two types of search algorithms you will see on the test.)

1. Both linear and binary searches try to find an element in a list.

2. Linear search starts with the first element, looks at each element one at a time to see if it is the correct element, and if it is, returns the location.

3. Sometimes you might see this search called a "sequential search" because of the way the search looks at each element, in sequence.

4. Each search algorithm has its advantages and drawbacks:

   ▶ Linear search is much easier to code, but is less efficient for larger sets.

   ▶ Binary search only works on ordered sets, but is better for larger sets.

Test Tip

For the End-of-Course Exam programming languages, the first element in a list is 1 and the last element in a list is equal to the length of the list. This may be different from the language that you learned. Since this part of the book is to help you get ready for the End-of-Course Exam, this is the approach you will see here to iterate through a list. Assume list[index] is the element in list at index and a return of −1 means that the target was not found.

5. Pseudocode for linear search might look something like this:

```
STEP 1: Ask person what they are trying to find.
STEP 2: Store this in a variable called TARGET.
STEP 3: Create and store 0 in a variable called index.
STEP 4: While index < length of list
        index = index + 1
        Compare TARGET to list[index]
          If TARGET = element
            return index
          else
            index = index + 1
STEP 5: return −1
```

    i.   So if a list has 10 elements, the search will take at most 10 loops to determine if the target is in the list, or not.

       ▸ If the list has n elements, the search will take at most n comparisons.

       ▸ This is why we say that this search is "on the order of" n or, using Big O notation, $O(n) = n$.

       ▸ The second name of this search should now make sense. Since $O(n) = n$ is a linear function, the name given to this search is "linear search."

    Note that there are no special requirements on the list to make linear search work. This is one way that linear search is different from binary search.

B. Binary search assumes that a list is already in order and takes advantage of this.

    1. Binary search is called "binary" because it repeatedly splits the list into two parts.

    2. After each loop of this search, half the list is removed.

    3. For each division by 2, if the result is not an integer, you can assume that it rounds up. The procedure that manages this is not shown. It is called *roundup*.

    4. You can assume that if the target is not found, the code should return −1.

5. Pseudocode for binary search might look something like this:

> STEP 1: Ask person what they are trying to find.
> STEP 2: Store this in a variable called TARGET.
> STEP 3: Create variables called low, high, and middle.
> STEP 4: low = 1.
> STEP 5: high = length of list.
> STEP 6: middle = roundUp((length of list)/2)
> STEP 7: While (low ≤ high)
> > if (list[middle] < TARGET)
> > > low = middle
> > else if (list[middle] > TARGET)
> > > high = middle
> > else if (list[middle]=TARGET)
> > > return middle
> > middle = roundUp((low + high)/2)
> STEP 8: return −1

Notice that this algorithm is more complicated to code. You do not need to worry about writing it from scratch, but it is important to notice why the list needs to be ordered for it to work.

6. Let's trace it through with the following short list of alphabetized items:

   i.   Assume that the list we are searching is: {"ANT", "BAT", "CAT", "DOG", "HORSE", "LION"}.

   ii. Our target (the element we want to find) is "DOG."

   iii. Stepping through the code, low = 1, high = 6, and middle = 6/2 = 3.

   iv. Since low < high, we enter the *while* loop.

   > list[middle] = list[3] = "CAT"
   > Since "CAT" < "DOG", the first *if* statement is true.
   > So low = 3.
   > middle = roundUp((3+6)/2) = roundUp(4.5) = 5
   > high is still 6

Notice how the list is now split in half.

> ▸ The new low is 3. The new high is 6.

> ▸ Since "DOG" cannot be in a position less than 3, we will not look at that lower half of the set again.

> ▸ Half of the set is eliminated in one loop!

v. Back to the *while* loop: low(3) is still less than high(6) so we loop again:

> list[middle] = list[5] = "HORSE"
> This time, "HORSE" > "DOG" so the *else if* statement is true.

> ▸ This time, high is modified to 5 and low remains at 3.

> ▸ Once again, the set is split in half and this time, the lower half remains.

> ▸ After the *else if* ends, middle = roundUp((3+5)/2) = 4.

vi. Again, we enter the *while* loop since low(3) is less than high(5):

list[middle] = list[4] = "DOG"

Since the third *else if* will be true, the procedure will return middle, which is 4.

Note that it took three loops to locate "DOG." In a sequential search, it would have taken four loops.

Test Tip

Try tracing the search for a different target. Tracing code or pseudocode takes practice. The more examples you practice before the End-of-Course Exam, the more likely you will find an approach to tracing that works for you.

C. Usually, in an ordered set, binary search is faster than a linear search.

1. On average, if the set has 16 elements, it would take 4 loops to find the target. Can you see why? Each loop eliminates half the set. So 16 elements would go to 8 elements in loop 1, 4 elements in loop 2, 2 elements in loop 3, and find the target in loop 4.

2. Binary search would take about 5 loops for 32 elements, 6 loops for 64, and so on.

3. For *n* elements, binary search will take $\log_2 n$ loops to find the target.

4. So, for binary search $O(n) = \log_2 n$. This is a logarithmic search algorithm.

5. In an ordered set, the larger *n* gets, the larger the advantage of using binary search instead of linear search:

Size of set	Number of loops in Linear Search	Number of loops in Binary Search
8	8	3
64	64	6
256	256	8
n	*n*	$\log_2(n)$

EXAMPLE 3:

A list called dogs contains the names of dogs found in a park. A person wants to write a procedure to return the location if the dog name is in dogs and −1 if the dog name is not in dogs.

The person has the following procedures available to create this new procedure called findDog:

Procedure	Explanation
`sort(list)`	Sorts `list` in alphabetical order and returns the resulting list
`binarySearch(target, list)`	Performs a binary search to return the location of `target` in `list` if `target` is in the `list`, −1 otherwise
`linearSearch(target, list)`	Performs a linear search to return the location of `target` in `list` if `target` is in `list`, −1 otherwise

The procedure will look like THIS:

```
PROCEDURE findDog(name, dogs)
{
   <instructions>
   RETURN (location)
}
```

Which of the following could not replace <instructions> to correctly implement this procedure?

(A) location = linearSearch(name, sort(dogs))

(B) location = binarySearch(name, dogs)

(C) location = binarySearch(name, sort(dogs))

(D) location = linearSearch(name, dogs)

Answer: (B)

To apply binary search, the list needs to be sorted. Linear search has no such requirement. Whether a list is sorted or not, the linear search algorithm looks at all elements in a list; so, either choice (A) or (D) would find the target correctly. However, choice (A) would take more time to do so due to the sorting algorithm being called first. Choice (C) correctly sorts before attempting binary search.

D. Explain the difference between an algorithm that will run in reasonable time or not.

1. Linear search and binary search are examples of algorithms that run in reasonable time.

2. Optimization problems ("find the best," "find the smallest") often cannot be solved in reasonable time, but approximations to the best solution can be solved in reasonable time.

3. If an algorithm is analyzed and it is determined that the number of comparisons can be modeled using a polynomial function or better, this means that the algorithm will run in reasonable time.

   i. Polynomial efficiency means that as the size of the set increases, the number of comparisons might be the same, doubled, cubed, etc.

      ▶ If the number of comparisons increases in proportion to the size of the set, we say that is linear efficiency.

         – We could model it using Big O notation as follows: $O(n) = n$.

         – Linear search has this efficiency because linear search runs in reasonable time.

      ▶ If the number of comparisons increases by a power of, say 2, of the number of elements in the set, this is quadratic efficiency.

         – We could model it using the following Big O notation: $O(n) = n^2$.

         – Selection sort has this efficiency and since it is polynomial, it runs in reasonable time.

      ▶ Selection sort (with $O(n) = n^2$) requires more time than a linear search ($O(n) = n$), but both run in reasonable time since they are polynomial.

ii. An example of an efficiency that is better than polynomial is logarithmic.

  ▸ Logarithmic efficiency means that as the size of the set increases, the number of comparisons required increases by the logarithm of that size. This would mean logarithmic functions require less comparisons than a linear function for large sets.

    – Suppose that n is the number of elements in a set and that $n = 1000$.

      1. In an algorithm with linear efficiency (so $O(n) = n$), 1000 elements would require 1000 comparisons (on average).

      2. For a logarithmic function, $O(n) = \log(n)$.

      Assuming that we are talking about a common logarithm ($O(n) = \log_{10}(n)$) then $\log(1000) = 3$. The difference is extreme!

  ▸ A binary search has logarithmic efficiency.

    – Binary search has an efficiency of $\log_2(n)$. Since this means it requires fewer comparisons than even a linear search, it definitely runs in reasonable time.

    – In a binary search, you assume that the set is ordered.

    – In the ordered set, you look for the target by splitting the set into smaller sets.

E. Explain the difference between solvable and unsolvable problems.

  1. An unsolvable problem cannot be solved using any algorithm.

  2. A solvable problem can be solved using an algorithm.

    i. Some solvable problems run in reasonable time (efficiency is better than a polynomial) and some solvable problems will not run in reasonable time.

F. Explain the difference between decidable and undecidable problems.

1. An undecidable problem may have a solution for some situations, but not all.

2. A decidable problem has a solution for all situations.

3. Therefore, a decidable problem may or may not run in reasonable time but is solvable.

4. An undecidable problem may or may not run in reasonable time and it may or may not be solvable.

Key Topics Related to Programming

I. OVERVIEW

A. About 20 percent of the End-of-Course Exam questions (15 of the 74 questions) will focus on programming.

B. In addition, the Create Performance Task is focused on improving your skills in this area.

II. WHAT IS PROGRAMMING?

A. *Programming* is the act of teaching a computer what you want it to do.

B. A program often involves translating pseudocode to actual code.

C. Creating a program involves many stages that include:

1. learning a language.

2. planning the program you want to create.

3. writing the program in that language.

4. debugging:

    i.   making sure that the computer understands what you mean (if it does not, this is likely a syntax error).

    ii. checking that the program works as intended (if it does not, this might be a semantic error).

5. experimenting with different approaches to a program:

    i.   Syntax and semantic errors are solved differently.

      ▸ To fix syntax errors, you may need to refer to program documentation to check the way you are writing your program.

      ▸ To fix semantic errors, you may need to display what is going on in the program or consider redesigning your program.

6. reflecting before planning the next iteration (steps) of the program.

7. Repeat steps 2 through 5 until the program works as intended.

III. WHAT YOU NEED TO KNOW AND UNDERSTAND ABOUT PROGRAMMING

A. Programs are developed for many reasons and depend on the goal of the programmer.

B. There are four main reasons programs are created:

1. for creative expression

2. to satisfy a curiosity

3. to create new knowledge

4. to solve a problem for an individual, group, organization, or society

C. When a program is developed, the following statements are true:

1. A program may have inputs or outputs that are visual (images, words, video), audible (sound), or tactile (sensors, robot movements).

2. The program's purpose is related to the approach (language, methods, and standards) used to create it.

    i. If a program is created for one person, the methods and standards may only work for that person.

        ▸ If that person wants to involve others, they may need to modify their design and/or approach.

        ▸ If that person wants to scale up to larger distribution, the program may need significant changes.

    ii. If a program is created for widespread distribution, methods and standards must be scalable. This means:

        ▸ The design needs to be clear so that many people can understand it. Often helpful are:

            – flowcharts

            – written documentation of purpose, inputs, and outputs of program and key pieces of program

        ▸ The methods and standards used should be consistent throughout the program. Often helpful are:

            – language documentation (for the language used in the End-of-Course Exam, refer to your Exam Reference Sheet)

            – standards documents

3. A program may do more than was originally planned.

    i. The final outcome of a program may be better than what you thought when you started the program.

    ii. The program may become a "piece" of a larger program, or the beginning of a new idea or focus.

    iii. The results of the program may be shared with others and could impact individuals, organizations, and society.

4. As computing advances, so does our ability to use programming to think creatively in many fields.

D. The process of creating a program is iterative and incremental.

1. It is *incremental* since you can create and test small pieces of code at a time.

2. It is *iterative* since each piece that you add impacts the program.

   i.   When working with others, each piece added needs to be managed carefully.

   ii. Programmers need to accept the approved design, but they can be creative in their approach to solving problems.

3. If the small pieces (components) are verified to be correct, the overall program is more likely to be correct.

   i.   Incremental testing after adding components into a program helps verify overall program correctness.

   ii. A programmer's skill, style, and knowledge impacts how a problem is solved.

4. As incremental or iterative changes happen, programmers need to be careful managing these changes. If managed carefully, less time will be spent on debugging, and the program will likely work as intended. Here are some ideas for managing these changes:

   i.   Have consistent documentation. Be sure that programmers put comments into code to define inputs, outputs, and intent of components of code.

   ii. Spend time on program design. Programmers should decide on the overall goal of the program and how each component should work together to accomplish this.

   iii. Be sure to communicate with the people who will use the program. Concerns from users of the program need to be addressed in design and documentation.

   iv. Consider collaboration. Programmers work with others for the following reasons:

   ▸ to break down a program into smaller, more manageable pieces

> ‣ to have more ideas in solving problems while programming

> ‣ to make errors easier to find and correct

E. A *program* is how an algorithm is implemented (understood by a computer).

F. The following are always true in a program:

1. Instructions are processed sequentially (in order).

2. Instructions may involve variables which may change or be output from the program.

3. A program automates processes in a computer.

   i.   These processes use memory, a central processing unit (CPU), input, and output.

   ii. Each process may execute by itself or with other processes.

   iii. A process may execute on one or several CPUs.

   iv. There are layers of abstraction to these processes. (See Appendix D for more details about these layers.)

4. Executable programs increase the scale of problems that can be addressed.

   i. A program can run multiple times, keep accurate results, and combine these results to improve learning and/or performance.

   ii. An algorithm may seem simple (such as finding the minimum), but by automating it you can save time dealing with future problems.

5. Procedures can help you organize your program.

   i. Procedures are named groupings of programming instructions.

   ii. Many common algorithms become procedures so they can be used by name rather than rewriting code.

    iii. Procedures may have parameters and return values.

- ▸ The use of a parameter (called *parameterization*) helps you to think of a problem more generally.

- ▸ If a procedure has a problem, you can test and fix it once instead of trying to fix it in multiple places of your code.

6. The type of data being input, output, or transformed in a procedure needs to be considered.

    i. Abstract Data Types (ADTs) are treated differently from numbers in a program.

- ▸ An ADT is any data type that is more complicated than a number.

- ▸ Lists and other collections are considered ADTs.

- ▸ A sprite or an object that you created while programming is another example of an ADT.

    ii. Mathematical operations are parts of many procedures.

- ▸ Examples of mathematical operations are addition, subtraction, multiplication, division, modulus, and Boolean operations such as AND, OR, or NOT.

- ▸ When the results are stored in a memory location, the actual value stored may be limited by the amount of memory available for that data type.

  - – Real numbers are approximated by floating point representations that may not be exact (for example, ⅓ will be approximated).

  - – Each programming language handles this storage differently and often does not let you know that any approximation has happened.

    iii. Boolean variables are true or false.

- ▸ The use of Boolean operations such as AND, OR, and NOT helps to develop correct programs.

> ▸ The result of Boolean operations becomes the input for conditionals such as an *if*-statement or a *while*-statement.

7. There are some procedures that are included with a language.

   i. Documentation for a language includes information about Application Program Interfaces (APIs) and libraries that would help simplify tasks.

   ii. List operations (such as *add, remove,* and *search*) are common in many programs.

   iii. APIs allow software components to communicate in a language.

> *The best way to learn about programming is to actually do it! You need to experiment, make mistakes, and learn from them. There are several languages that you could choose, and there are several online resources that you could use to learn. See Appendix B for a list of possible languages to experiment with.*

IV. WHAT YOU NEED TO DO WITH PROGRAMMING

A. In the End-of-Course Exam, you will need to read a program written in the exam "language" and determine if it did what the programmer meant for it to do. The best way to practice this is to do the following:

1. Program in an actual language and learn from your mistakes.

   i. Choose projects that will help you to learn. The most meaningful projects

   > ▸ will interest you;
   >
   > ▸ will challenge you;
   >
   > ▸ will help you to solve a problem; or
   >
   > ▸ have been created by someone else to teach you.

195

Note: If this is your first programming experience and you are doing this course independently, a block-based language may be your best choice. (Refer to Appendix B for a list of possible languages.) The Create Performance Task is an example of a task you complete while learning a language.

Test Tip

Refer to Chapter 17 for practice with many questions designed to help you master the programming language used on the End-of-Course Exam.

EXAMPLE 1:

Suppose you would like to create a procedure to find and print the smallest item in the list. The procedure might look like this:

```
PROCEDURE printMin(theList)
{
   min 0
   FOR EACH item IN theList
   {
      if (min > item)
      {
       min ← item
      }
   }
   DISPLAY ("smallest item in list is " + min)
}
```

In what situation would this procedure fail to correctly display the minimum?

(A) In no situation; this procedure works as intended

(B) In all situations; this procedure will DISPLAY the maximum, not the minimum

(C) If every item in the list is positive

(D) If every item in the list is negative

Answer: (C)

If every item is positive, then it will never satisfy the condition "min > item." The min will remain set to 0. To avoid this, when finding the minimum, the test variable (min for this example) should be set to the maximum allowable value. Alternatively, you could send it to an element of the list.

B. Read logic and math written in a program and determine what the output or behavior will be.

EXAMPLE 2A:

Which of the following code segments will correctly swap the values of variables x and y? Select **two** answers.

```
(A) x ← y
    y ← x

(B) temp ← x
    x ← y
    y ← temp

(C) temp ← y
    y ← x
    x ← temp

(D) temp ← x
    y ← temp
    x ← y
```

Answers: (B), (C)

This is a common algorithm you probably have seen in programming examples. To swap, you need a temporary variable to hold the value of one of the variables so that value is not lost. The order that you pass parameters is important. Pseudocode for the swap algorithm is:

```
create temporary variable
put one value into temporary variable
reassign stored variable to new value
since original value is held in temporary variable it is fine
note that now both variables have the same value
reassign second variable to value stored in temporary variable
```

EXAMPLE 2B:

In the procedure Mystery below, the parameter value is a positive number.

```
PROCEDURE Mystery(value)
{
  REPEAT UNTIL (value = 0)
  {
    if ((value MOD 2) = 0)
      value ← value - 2
    else
      value ← value - 3
  }
  RETURN value
}
```

Mystery is used in another program. Which of the following statements is true about what will happen when it is used?

(A) Using Mystery could cause an infinite loop.

(B) Using Mystery will never cause an infinite loop.

(C) value will always be 0.

(D) value will always be a multiple of 2.

Answer: (A)

If Mystery(1) were called (if the parameter value were set to 1), then value would be reassigned to –2 in the loop. This would cause an infinite loop since value could never be 0. This problem could be avoided by using the condition (value <= 0) in the REPEAT loop.

In all other calls, Mystery would return 0.

C. Show that you understand why and how to define procedures for a purpose in a program. Some common reasons to create a procedure are:

1. to reorganize an existing program.

i.   Breaking down logical or mathematical concepts into smaller procedures can make it easier to read and/or debug a program.

ii. By creating a procedure and naming it carefully, your code will be more readable.

2. to make an object or event happen in a program.

EXAMPLE 3:

Suppose you need to write a procedure called getMax(list) that accepts a list as a parameter and returns the largest number in the list. You can assume that list has at least one item in it and that all numbers in list are positive.

Which of the following statements is false about this algorithm?

(A) It involves sequencing, selection, and iteration.

(B) Order matters, a conditional statement will be used, and a loop will be used.

(C) This procedure is an example of an abstraction and/ or algorithm you will need to explain in the Create Performance Task *and* the End of Course Assessment.

(D) You need to see how this is implemented before deciding to use it in code.

Answer: (D)

Choices (A) and (B) are equivalent statements. Choice (C) is true. Since sequencing, selection, iteration, and math/logic are involved, this algorithm would meet the minimum requirement for the Create Performance Task for the required algorithm. Since details are abstracted away (you do not need to see the algorithm to use it), it helps manage complexity in code. Therefore, it would meet the requirement for the required abstraction. This also explains why choice (D) is false.

Key Topics Related to Abstraction

 I. **OVERVIEW**

   A. You can expect about 19 percent of the End-of-Course Exam questions (14 of the 74 questions) to focus on abstraction.

   B. In addition, the Create Performance Task has a prompt (Prompt 2d) related to this topic (see Chapter 14).

 II. **WHAT IS ABSTRACTION?**

   A. An abstraction has two roles in a program:

     1. It reduces or removes details to help you to understand something new.

     2. It helps you manage the details and code of a program.

   B. There are many layers to any abstraction.

     1. In general, when it comes to abstraction, "less is more." The less detail, the more abstract.

III. **WHAT YOU NEED TO KNOW AND UNDERSTAND ABOUT ABSTRACTION**

   A. Abstractions are described in terms of level or layer.

     1. A higher-level abstraction is more general.

2. A lower-level abstraction is more specific.

3. Lower-level abstractions can be combined to make higher-level abstractions.

4. See Appendix D for a list of abstractions in terms of their level.

B. When designing a program, programmers use and generate many examples of abstraction to study, test, or create something that may eventually be real. Some of these include:

1. The program may be written to model (or simulate) an actual situation. For example, an engineering company builds a program that models a radar system and the different ways that system will be used in order to verify that it is going to perform as needed.

2. The program may contain objects designed to represent an actual object in our world. For example, an animation studio wants to make a movie that shows water that looks real.

3. The program may be written to test a hypothesis that cannot be tested or simulated in real life. For example, a company wants to know the result of one flu shot versus another flu shot being given to an entire population.

C. Any program contains examples of abstraction.

1. All digital data is an abstraction.

2. All data eventually becomes binary digits (bits) that the computer interprets.

3. The source of these bits could have been any of the following:

    i.   hexadecimal digits

    ii. decimal digits

    iii. color codes

    iv. characters

    v. operations

    vi. programming commands

  4. Bits are grouped to represent a color.

    i. "11111111, 11111111, 11111111" could be a color in binary.

    ii. In the hexadecimal number system, you would read "FF, FF, FF."

    iii. In the decimal number system, you would read, "255, 255, 255."

    iv. On a computer screen, you would see this as "white."

D. The use of the abstraction tells you information about the layer you want to see.

  1. This is true for every symbol, language, and part of a computer.

  2. This is true no matter what you are trying to model or understand.

E. Abstractions occur in hardware and software applications. (See Appendix D.)

  1. A program created to solve or understand a problem is an abstraction of that problem.

  2. A program simulating a game is an abstraction of that game.

  3. A procedure that automates an important behavior in a program is an abstraction of that behavior.

  4. A data structure, such as a list, models a collection of items that need to be grouped together to simulate a real situation (for example, a list of card objects simulates a deck). Ultimately, this structure is stored as bits.

  5. A motherboard contains a CPU and memory. Within each of these are several details such as chips or logic gates.

F. Converting data often comes at a cost.

   1. Some data cannot be converted without loss.

   2. Some numbers we see often (such as ⅓) cannot be stored in a computer.

   3. To teach a computer in a language it understands, infinite mathematical concepts are modeled by finite representations of infinity.

   4. Some numbers need to be rounded to be stored.

      i. If the memory allocated for that number is too small to hold the result, these rounded numbers are an approximation of the exact value.

      ii. This is called an overflow error.

G. Three number systems are used in a computer program. These are:

   1. decimal (our number system)

   2. binary (base 2)

   3. hexadecimal (base 16)

H. The hexadecimal number system is used to fit more data into less digits.

IV. ABSTRACTIONS ARE USEFUL IN COMPUTER SCIENCE

A. Abstractions provide a common language to describe parts of a computer.

B. They are also a tool in programming and in simulating our reality.

C. Through an abstraction, such as a program, we can try out hypotheses without real-world constraints.

D. Through our design decisions, we decide which details to keep or remove.

E. Models and simulations are created on a computer to form and refine hypotheses (educated guesses) about an object or phenomena that cannot be understood or tested easily in the physical world.

F. The time required to run a simulation depends on the following:

1. the level of detail and quality of the model

2. the software and hardware being used for the simulation.

V. WHAT YOU NEED TO DO WITH ABSTRACTION

A. Identify and/or use layers of abstraction to serve a purpose in a program.

EXAMPLE 1:

Suppose you are creating a program to model a solitaire card game that you can play on the computer.

1A. What are some objects in a card game that you will likely want to simulate?

1B. What are some important actions in a card game?

1C. What are some hypotheses you could use the game to test?

Answers

1A. A card (depending on the game, you may just want the card to be a number, or maybe you need to know rank or suit); a deck (could be a list of card objects)

1B. Knowing if you won or lost, dealing a card, shuffling the deck

1C. If I play this game 100 times, I believe I will win 40 times. (You could run the simulation in a loop and keep track of the number of times you won or lost.)

Test Tip

Multiple-choice prompts will ask you about different situations. Do not worry about how familiar you are with the context. It does not matter if you have experience with the situation or not. Focus on the connection to the topic. In Example 1, you are asked about abstractions, so think about the key aspects of any card game. Look to remove details.

B. Recognize examples of overflow errors.

EXAMPLE 2:

Which of the following is most likely an example of an overflow error?

(A) (x ← 1/3)

(B) (x ← 1/0)

(C) list ← | 1, 2, 3 |
    i ← 0

    REPEAT 4 TIMES
        i ← i + 1
        DISPLAY list i

(D) i ← 0
    REPEAT UNTIL NOT i = 0
        i ← i * 100

Answer: (A)

An overflow error is an error caused by a number being too large for the memory allocated. For the End-of-Course Exam, you can assume that ⅓ will be handled as floating point division. Storing ⅓ will involve rounding since there is a finite number of bits used to represent any number and ⅓ is an infinitely repeating decimal. Note that each programming language manages this differently, so you should practice these nuances before the End-of-Course Exam.

Some key points from Example 2:

> All of these errors (including choice A) are common semantic errors. They would not be caught until you run the program.
>
> Choice (B) is an example of dividing by 0.
>
> Choice (C) is an example of an Off-By-One-Error (OBOE) since the loop attempts to use an index that is too large for the list.
>
> Choice (D) is an example of an infinite loop. i is 0. Multiplying by any number will not change this, so the loop will not be broken.

C. Be able to convert to and from positive integer values stored in any of the following number systems: binary, hexadecimal, and decimal. (See Appendix C for more information on how to convert between number systems.)

EXAMPLE 3

3A. Convert 167 to the binary number system.

3B. Convert 362 to the hexadecimal number system.

3C. Convert 167 to the hexadecimal number system.

Answers

3A. Remember that binary numbers have place values that are powers of 2.

decimal number 167 $= 128 + 32 + 4 + 2 + 1$

$= 1(128) + 0(64) + 1(32) + 0(16) + 0(8) + 1(4) + 1(2) + 1(1)$

$= 1(2^7) + 0(2^6) + 1(2^5) + 0(2^4) + 0(2^3) + 1(2^2) + 1(2^1) + 1(2^0)$

$=$ binary number 10100111

3B. Hexadecimal digits are powers of 16.

decimal number 362 $= 256 + 106$

$= 256 + 6(16) + 10$

$= 1(256) + 6(16) + 10(1)$

$= 1(16^2) + 6(16^1) + 10(16^0)$

$=$ hexadecimal number 16A

3C. This as a similar problem to Example 3B. You could choose to do the arithmetic and verify that you are able to get the same answer using powers of 16. Instead, let's use the fact that we already have 167 in binary.

Since decimal number 167 = binary number 10100111, we can see each nibble (collection of 4 bits) as containing a power of 16 since $16 = 2^4$. Looking at the left-most nibble: 1010, 1010 = 8 + 2 = 10. Binary number 10 converted to hexadecimal number A. Looking at the right-most nibble: binary number 0111, 0111 = 111 = 4 + 2 + 1 = hexadecimal number 7.

So, binary number 10100111 = hexadecimal number A7.

D. Be able to recognize the difference between a low-level and high-level abstraction, and order abstractions based on their level.

See Appendix D for a table of abstractions you can expect to see on your End-of-Course Exam. You do not need to memorize this list, but you do need to know how the abstractions are related to each other. Multiple-choice questions will provide enough details so that, as long as you can see abstractions and/or convert to binary and/or hexadecimal numbers, you will be able to answer the questions.

EXAMPLE 4

4A. ASCII is the encoding scheme used to represent characters as a number. An example of this scheme is the uppercase letter "B" represented by "42" in hexadecimal digits. How would the letter be represented in its lowest level of abstraction?

4B. RGB (Red, Green, Blue) Values are used to encode color as a number. The first RGB encoding scheme used 8 bits (3 for red, 3 for green, 2 for blue). How many different colors (called a palette) could be created with this scheme?

4C. ("Sneak Peek"). The current RGB scheme uses 24 bits per color. It is called "True Color" because the large number of colors in this palette make images created with it look more real.

Which of the following best describes the result of using 24-bit RGB encoding instead of 8-bit RGB encoding?

(A) 3 times as many values can be represented

(B) 2^{16} times as many values can be represented

(C) 16^3 as many values can be represented

(D) 16 times as many values can be represented

Answers

4A. The lowest level abstraction of a number is binary. 42 in hexadecimal digits is 01000010 or 1000010. Since 4 = 0100 and 2 is 0010, recall that you can convert directly between hexadecimal and binary digits 4 bits at a time.

4B. 8 bits means that in each bit there are 2 possibilities (1 or 0). So there are 2^8 possible combinations. $2^8 = 256$, so there are 256 colors possible in the RGB palette.

- The colors would be represented by decimal values from 0 to 255.

- To save digits, colors are often stored in hexadecimal digits from 0 to FF.

- Eventually, at its lower level, colors would be represented in binary digits, or bits from 00000000 to 11111111.

4C. (B) 24-bit RGB encoding means 2^{24} colors can be represented. The color palette has 2^{24} distinct colors. This is $2^{24}/2^8 = 2^{(24-8)} = 2^{16}$ times as many colors as the 8-bit RGB palette.

E. Handle multiple versions of abstractions in a programming language.

Test Tip

Refer to Chapter 17 for practice with many versions of abstractions related to the programming language used on the End-of-Course Exam. These include logic gates, robot movement, and related algorithms.

Key Topics Related to Data and Information

 I. OVERVIEW

A. You can expect about 18 percent of the End-of-Course Exam questions (13 out of 74) to focus on data and information.

B. In addition, the Explore Performance Task has a writing prompt (Prompt 2d) that focuses on this topic (see Chapter 6).

 II. WHAT IS DATA AND/OR INFORMATION?

A. Data and information are inputted, outputted, and/or transformed within a computing innovation.

B. Data scientists use computing and existing data to create new understandings. This is an essential field in our world because of the following:

1. We have more data than ever available to us for entertainment, decision-making, and problem-solving.

2. As this data increases, so does our need to understand patterns and display conclusions.

C. By studying computer science, you will notice that data and information

1. contribute knowledge to the world.

2. require creation and use of computing tools.

3. are constantly being transformed.

III. WHAT YOU NEED TO KNOW AND UNDERSTAND ABOUT DATA AND INFORMATION

A. People use programs to process information and to learn about the world that the data describes.

1. Some of that learning is related to finding patterns or testing hypotheses.

   i. Computer scientists design programs to check these hypotheses. Sometimes, as a result of new learning, computer scientists modify these programs and/or make new hypotheses.

   ii. Data often needs to be combined in creative ways to check for patterns. Computers help in this process by helping users

   ▶ combine data sources.

   ▶ cluster data.

   ▶ classify data.

   ▶ find trends in data.

   iii. Computers are a tool to help people translate and transform data, leading to discoveries that would not have been possible without the computer.

2. Collaboration plays an important role in using computing tools to solve data problems.

   i. By involving others, programmers gain:

   ▶ multiple perspectives to ask new questions or find new patterns.

   ▶ additional knowledge and skills in using tools to display results and/or manipulate data.

   ▶ assistance when working with data sets that are too large to process independently.

   ii. Communication is essential to be sure that the description of the data is accurate.

3. Explaining knowledge learned from data is a skill that needs to be practiced.

   i. Computing tools can help you tell a story about data. This is required to complete your Explore Performance Task artifact (see Chapter 3).

B. Computing can lead to new discoveries from data sets.

   1. You can use computing tools to pull information from data.

      i. The size of a data set impacts the way in which it is processed and the information that can be learned from that set.

         ‣ A larger set may provide a more "real world" view, but it may also require more processing than is possible, or it may be difficult to access the information within that set.

         ‣ A smaller set may need to be expanded in size to create a new conclusion.

      ii. Computing tools are essential for

         ‣ searching data.

         ‣ displaying data.

         ‣ processing data.

         ‣ storing data.

   2. Computing tools can help you discover/explain connections and trends.

IV. WHAT YOU NEED TO DO WITH DATA AND INFORMATION

A. Find patterns and make guesses (hypotheses) in the following ways:

   1. Use tools to provide evidence of these patterns and/or guesses.

   2. Explain how large data sets require a different set of tools to find patterns and make guesses.

EXAMPLE 1:

A scientist is using an application to study flowers that are in bloom over a large geographic area. The application is capable of:

- translating an image of a flower to its scientific name.

- creating a database of that flower's image, its name, a timestamp of when the image was taken, and the flower's location when the image was taken.

1A. Which of the following questions about flowers could NOT be answered using only the data collected within this database?

(A) What is the most frequent flower type in a geographic area?

(B) When flowers are most likely to be in bloom in a geographic area?

(C) How has climate change impacted the spread of a particular type of flower?

(D) What time of day are images of flowers most likely to be taken?

1B. The scientist encourages many people to contribute to improving and using this application using their smart phones for the purpose of studying patterns of flower growth over many years. How might she describe her data collection process to others?

I. This is an example of *crowdsourcing*. Many people are improving the application.

II. This is an example of *citizen science*. Many people are contributing to the database.

III. This is an example of an application that uses *metadata*. The database has a timestamp for each data point collected.

(A) I and II

(B) I, II, and III

(C) II only

(D) None of these

Answers:

1A. (C) To determine climate change, multiple time samples over long periods of time would be necessary. We do not know how long this study has taken place.

1B. (B) These are all examples of ways a scientist might describe the collection process. Each vocabulary term is one you need to know in relation to data and databases, and their applications.

B. Analyze how data representation, storage, security, and transmission all require computational manipulation of information.

EXAMPLE 2:

Refer to Example 1. What is a likely decision that was made about the data stored on this database? Select two answers.

(A) It is likely that this database uses lossy compression for the GPS coordinates of each flower.

(B) It is likely that the server that contains this database is the scientist's personal computer.

(C) It is likely that the database uses lossy compression for the flower images.

(D) It is not likely that the database is backed up multiple times each day.

Answers: (C), (D)

Answer (A) is incorrect because GPS coordinates are numerical. Compression would more likely be used on an image where it would save more space. Choice (B) is incorrect because it is not likely that the database is housed on a personal computer because of space and security concerns. Choice (D) is correct because it is very likely that the database is backed up multiple times per day to prevent data from being lost or corrupted.

Notice how one specific example leads to several related multiple-choice questions. This is typical for questions in the Data and Information category. Since the context of questions takes time to set up, several questions may be related to one situation. This is why it is best to answer questions in sequence in a chain of questions related to one situation. Once you understand the context, answer all of the questions related to it. Jumping around will only delay and likely confuse you.

C. Remember that in the Explore Performance Task, you need to explain

1. the data type itself.

2. how the data is consumed, produced, or transformed.

3. a storage, privacy, or security concern.

4. how that concern leads to a consequence.

   i. The concern must be

      ▸ identified as a storage, privacy, or security concern;

      ▸ explained with enough detail that the reader understands what the concern is; and

      ▸ connected to a consequence of that concern. You must clarify what could happen as a result of this concern.

Key Topics Related to the Internet

I. OVERVIEW

A. About 13 percent of the End-of-Course Exam questions (10 of the 74 questions) will focus on the Internet.

B. There are many new words and concepts that you need to be familiar with to score well on these questions.

II. WHAT IS THE INTERNET?

A. The Internet is a collection of systems that are connected worldwide using software and hardware.

B. All parts of the Internet have agreed-upon *protocols* (ways of communicating) and *addresses* (ways to find hardware on the Internet) that allow the system to work.

C. The Internet has revolutionized communication and collaboration worldwide.

D. Due to the open and trust-based nature of the Internet, cybersecurity is an important concern.

III. WHAT YOU NEED TO KNOW AND UNDERSTAND ABOUT THE INTERNET

A. The Internet is governed by protocols.

1. To connect to the Internet, a device needs an Internet Protocol (IP) address.

    i. The Domain Name System (DNS) translates domain names to IP addresses.

- Domain names are human-readable addresses. An example of a domain name is "rea" for "rea.com."

- Domain names are entered into a browser such as Google Chrome, Mozilla Firefox, or Safari.

    ii. The Domain Name System was created to make it easier for people to access information via the Internet.

- The Domain Name System translates the text (domain name) you enter into a browser into numbers (IP addresses).

- IP addresses are strings of numbers that are not easily understood by a person looking at the address.

- The way IP addresses are handled and stored is called "Internet Protocol."

2. There are two main Internet Protocols you need to be familiar with: IPv4 and IPv6.

    i. In "IPv4," an IP address was 4 bytes (32 bits) in length. Since 1 bit has 2 options (1 or 0), 4 bytes (32 bits) would allow for 2^{32} or approximately 4 million addresses.

    ii. Since the creation of IPv4, the number of devices that need IP addresses has increased.

    iii. To accommodate this increase, IPv6 was created to handle the routing of more devices.

    iv. IP addresses in IPv6 are 16 bytes (128 bits) in length.

    v. What does IPv6 really provide in terms of addresses? Here is the arithmetic to compare:

- Recall from number i above, that each bit has 2 options, 1 or 0. 128 bits means that there are 2^{128} or approximately 3.4×10^{38} different addresses available in IPv6.

- Comparing the number of addresses in IPv6 to IPv4, $(2^{128})/(2^{32}) = 2^{96}$. This is approximately 8×10^{28}.

> ‣ There are approximately 8×10^{28} times (80 octillion) as many addresses available in IPv6 when compared to IPv4.

3. There are several other protocols that control how devices communicate on the Internet.

    i.   All protocols are overseen by the Internet Engineering Task Force (IETF).

    ii. Other protocols include:

> ‣ Hypertext transfer protocol (HTTP)
>
> ‣ Internet protocol (IP)
>
> ‣ Voice Over Internet Protocol (VOIP)
>
> ‣ Real-time Transport Protocol (RTP)
>
> ‣ Simple Mail Transfer Protocol (SMTP)
>
> ‣ Transfer Control Protocol (TCP)

B. The Internet is managed by hierarchies.

1. The Internet was created to be hierarchical, which means it is a structure with many levels, each having a specific purpose. It is important to understand the levels and roles related to the Internet.

2. To understand the hierarchical nature of the Internet, let's look at a "real world" example of a hierarchical system: addressing an envelope for mailing a letter.

    i.   When you send a letter to someone, the envelope looks like this:

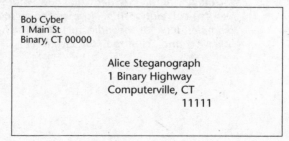

```
Bob Cyber
1 Main St
Binary, CT 00000

              Alice Steganograph
              1 Binary Highway
              Computerville, CT
                        11111
```

> ‣ When you look at this envelope, you know that Bob is the sender and Alice is the receiver of the envelope. (The fact that an envelope is filled out similarly each time allows you to know this.) This is an example of a protocol.

ii. The U.S. postal system is hierarchical in the way in which the mail is delivered:

> ‣ The post office that receives this letter looks first at the zip code to identify the town and state of the receiving post office. The letter is sent there.

> ‣ Once there, it is sent to the post office that services mail to Binary Highway.

> ‣ Once on that route, the mail carrier will drop the letter at number 1.

> ‣ Whoever lives at number 1 is responsible for being sure that Alice receives Bob's letter.

3. Protocols and hierarchies go hand-in-hand.

i. At all levels of a hierarchy, protocols are followed.

ii. By making these protocols public and using hierarchies to control them, the Internet has evolved to be a network of systems that can be accessed, used, and modified by all of us.

Test Tip

Analogies like addressing an envelope to explain the meaning of a hierarchy and to see how hierarchies and protocols are interconnected are examples of abstraction. The abstraction here was created so that, before you see the details and vocabulary of the Internet, you know what to notice in a hierarchical relationship. Now, when you read the following examples, look for the indicators of hierarchy: (1) structure, (2) levels, and (3) purpose at each level.

4. Examples of hierarchies that are part of the design of the Internet.

    i.   Hierarchical Example 1: IP addresses

        ▸ IP addresses are hierarchical. Thus, the order of the digits in an IP address matters.

        ▸ The image below shows the conversion of an IPv4 address from binary digits to decimal digits.

        ▸ Remember, in IPv4, an IP address is 4 bytes (32 bits) long.

Example of IPv4 Address

	FIRST PART	SECOND PART	THIRD PART
binary	11110000.11011011	11000011	00111100
decimal	240, 219	195	60

    – The first part of the address ("11110000.11011011" in binary, or "240, 219" in decimal) provides the network address (comparable to the "City, State" on the envelope example).

        a. The network is the system that contains the smaller systems that connect to the computer you are trying to find. This is sometimes called the "site prefix."

        b. On a network, the site prefix is given by the Internet Service Provider (ISP).

    – The second part of the address (195, in decimal) provides the sub-network, also called *subnet* (comparable to the street and street number on the envelope). This is a more specific section of the network.

- The third part of the address (60, in decimal) is the host (comparable to the person/persons addressed on the envelope).

  a. The host is the computer you are trying to reach.

  b. Notice that the more you move to the right, the more private (local) the information becomes.

    • Moving to the right on an IP address is similar to moving closer to the name on an envelope.

    • The left part of the IP address is publicly set up, while the right part is private to your network.

Your End-of-Course Exam will have questions related to IP addresses. For the exam, you do not need to know the specifics of each type of IP address. You do, however, need to know how to convert between binary and decimal number systems. (See Appendix C.)

▸ IPv6 was the solution to an overflow problem that happened when the number of IP addresses needed exceeded what IPv4 could support.

  - An IPv6 address consists of 128 bits. It is normally written as 8 groups of 4 hexadecimal digits.

    a. Remember that each hexadecimal digit is 4 bits.

    b. 8 x (4 hexadecimal digits x 4 bits/hexadecimal digit) = 8 x 16 bits = 128 bits.

  - IPv6 addresses are usually written in hexadecimal notation.

  - An example of an IPv6 address is shown below, with an explanation of what each part means in a typical address.

Example of IPv6 Address

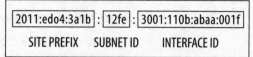

- The top line of the address may not look much larger, but consider that subnet "ID 12fe" (see center of image above) in hexadecimal digits is equal to:

  4862 in decimal digits

  0001 0010 1111 1110 in binary digits (or bits)

- Just as in IPv4, as you move to the right in the address, you get closer to the network.

- The site prefix is generally public knowledge, while the subnet ID and the interface ID is privately known on your network.

ii. Hierarchical Example 2: The Domain Name System

- ▶ Uniform Resource Locators (URLs) must conform to the Domain Name System, which was invented to make it possible for people to remember addresses.

- ▶ URLs are text-based names of websites; they are human-readable web addresses.

- ▶ The URL has the correct language, words, and system to deliver messages online from and to any connected device.

- ▶ An example of a URL is: *http://www.rea.com.*

  - – *http* stands for "Hypertext Transfer Protocol." This is the protocol that tells computers how to view information. It is similar to the flag on your mailbox that helps you and the mail deliverer communicate. *http* is a language with understood meaning.

- *https* stands for "Hypertext Transfer Protocol Secure." This adds an extra layer of security when browsing online.

- *www* stands for "World Wide Web." While entering "www" does not generally impact the information you access on a site, it might, depending on the way the site is set up. Whether you enter "http://www.rea.com" or "http://rea.com," you will most likely be directed to the same location.

- The domain name inside this URL is "rea." This name (combined with the extension) is what a person or a company purchased to use for a specific amount of time.

  - *com* is one of 270 top-level domain extensions that give you a clue about the purpose of the site. Another example of a top-level domain extension is *gov*, which, in the United States, identifies a government site.

iii. Hierarchical Example 3: The Internet and the Systems Built on It.

- Every device added to the Internet is given an IP (Internet Protocol) address that allows it to be used as a device on the Internet according to TCP/IP (Transmission Control Protocol/Internet Protocol).

- Each address is hierarchical. Many addresses can be reached using a Domain Name that follows the Domain Name System through a Uniform Resource Locator (URL).

- The hierarchical design and redundancy of the Internet has enabled it to grow into a worldwide innovation that changes in a hierarchical way to meet demands.

- Internet design and redundancy:

  - When data is sent from one part of the network to another, the data is broken into blocks of bits (packets) that contain enough information so that each packet can be re-routed if necessary.

- The way data moves through the system is controlled by several protocols that manage communication and security between hardware and software.

    a. The way data is broken and reassembled is called Transmission Control Protocol/Internet Protocol (TCP/IP).

    b. Routing between two points on the Internet is redundant since there is more than one way for data to move from one point to another.

    c. If a packet does not arrive, it may be rerouted.

- The data is secured through Secure Sockets Layer/Transport Layer Security (SSL/TLS) Protocols.

- The data is processed and viewable using Hypertext Transfer Protocol (HTTP).

C. The flow of data on the Internet is typically measured as *bandwidth*, which is calculated as follows:

1. The size of information being sent at any time is measured in bits.

2. The time between a request being sent and when it is received is called *latency*.

3. The *bandwidth* is the amount of bits sent over a fixed amount of time.

$$BANDWIDTH = \frac{AMOUNT\ OF\ BITS}{LATENCY}$$

4. To see the bandwidth of your current connection, use a tool such as *speedtest.net*.

D. Security (called *cybersecurity*) is an important concern for the Internet and all systems on it.

1. Cybersecurity is a balancing act between our need to communicate what we want to share and our need to protect information we do not want to share.

2. More people are using the Internet than ever before, making security an essential need. These communications often fall into the following categories:

    i. Social: Websites such as Facebook or Twitter allow people to share their views on society, read others' views, and connect with people.

    ii. Business- or school-related:

        ‣ To stay informed about your workplace or your school, you may need to regularly view websites such as your teacher's website or your school's website.

        ‣ You may also need to use the Internet to access your email or to contribute in another way, such as by blogging.

    iii. Financial: Many purchases are now being made online, rather than in retail stores. These purchases require your money to move from your account (credit card or your bank) to the vendor that sells the product.

    iv. Device-centric: A device, such as your phone, is accessing online data or software to run other applications or to provide information that you request.

3. As people continue to enjoy using the Internet, they also want to control how much information is being communicated. This occurs in the following ways:

    i. Every additional use of the Internet means new vulnerabilities to data.

    ii. There are protocols to ensure security when you access or when you share personal information on the Internet.

    iii. On the End-of-Course Exam, there are often questions related to data vulnerabilities created while using a browser.

SUMMARY OF VULNERABILITIES
THAT HAPPEN WHEN USING A BROWSER

Step	What is happening?	Security Issues:
1: You open up your browser so that you can type a website address.	Your computer verifies that you have an Internet Service Provider (ISP).	To have an ISP, the ISP can access your IP Address. This IP Address can be used to find the geographic location you are using to access the Internet.
2: You enter the name of a site as words into a browser.	A domain name server translates your words into an IP Address.	Your request is recorded by your browser.
3: Protocols used by your computer's browser will allow you to take advantage of the fact that you have connected to the Internet before.	File retrieval and file transfer protocols are a collection of protocols that allow you to view and/or download online information. *Caching* is used to make this process more efficient. If you have viewed the location before, it would be stored in your cache so it will be faster and easier to view again.	Your browser keeps a digital record of searches you have performed on any device using this browser called a search history. Your browser also creates small files called cookies when you interact with a website. These are used by other sites to identify you by your preferences and to create targeted advertisements.
4: You may need to type a password to access what you need at a location.	Their website has software that records your password to check that it is actually you.	Your browser may offer to save that password for you so you do not need to remember. Now, your password is in two places: your browser and their website.
5: You view a site and access the information you need.	Again, file retrieval and file transfer protocols are allowing you to interact with this site and new pages are added to your cache.	Cookies continue to be created depending on what you interact with while on this site.

4. Increasingly, people are giving permission to devices to access the Internet. As more and more devices are connected, this way of using the Internet is often called the "Internet of Things." This will only make security more essential.

   i. Beyond browsing, consider the following examples of where you are using the Internet:

       ▸ An application running on your phone: Facebook, Twitter, or a favorite game

       ▸ A source for saved media you deposited online: Dropbox or Google Drive

       ▸ An application that allows you to video chat: Facetime, Google Hangouts, Skype

       ▸ The place your phone accesses to learn which update is needed

       ▸ The software that allows the Global Positioning System (GPS) to provide frequent enough updates that you can get to where you want to go

       ▸ Your digital requests (such as the things you said to "Siri" or "Alexa") are translated to a request to a browser or another software application

   ii. As innovations that rely on the Internet increase, so do our needs to access this information.

   iii. As society begins to rely on the "Internet of Things" for daily decision-making, we also need protocols for each of those things to be open and secure.

5. To allow as many people as possible to have access to information and to protect their information, the Internet is "open." Important parts of this open nature include:

   i. The Domain Name System (DNS) is transparent.

       ▸ DNS was designed so that information could move quickly; it is not designed to be completely secure.

▸ By using an Internet Browser such as Google Chrome or Mozilla Firefox, people can enter addresses and be directed to a website without seeing the actual IP addresses used to route that request.

▸ You can use *whois.com/whois* or enter "WhoIs" inside the navigation bar of your favorite Internet browser to find public information about IP addresses and websites.

ii.   Communication protocols are public.

▸ Whenever a device is given an IP address, that device must communicate using accepted protocols.

▸ These protocols are open so that people designing these devices know and follow the "rules" of communication.

▸ The Internet Engineering Task Force (IETF) was created to manage key decisions about protocols.

▸ Many of these protocols are necessary to keep information secure.

▸ Protocols are evolving as we continue to change the way we use the Internet

iii. Cybersecurity relies on open standards.

▸ Cybersecurity consists of cryptography and protocols.

▸ Cryptography is the use of mathematical algorithms to encrypt and decrypt information.

▸ Each encryption and decryption involves the use of a key, a number that is used to hide or expose information.

▸ Certificate Authorities (CAs) issue digital certificates to validate that the key being used in an encryption is owned by the user.

▸ There are two types of encryption schemes: Symmetric encryption and Public Key encryption:

  – Symmetric encryption uses one key to encode and decode.

  – Public Key encryption uses two keys, one public and one private, to encode and decode. This is often called asymmetric encryption.

6. "Pretty Good Privacy" or "PGP" is used to describe the balance between people's desire for the fast transfer of information and the need for security.

  i. PGP often means that asymmetric encryption is used only when needed, because it requires more time. Here are two examples of this balance that you may see on the End-of-Course Exam:

  ▸ Credit cards with chips use asymmetric encryption in each transaction.

    – When the card is inserted into the reader, there is a delay. During the delay, a secret key and digital signature are assigned to the transaction that can only be issued through this chip for this transaction. The card chip is the only one with this key, making it the private key.

    – Anyone can have your card number, your name, and even the security code on the back of the card. This information (along with the bank information) is public. But without the chip, no one can get the private key.

    – The private key acts as a lock around access to your funds. Access to account information does not mean access to funds without your permission. Anyone can use the public key to view an account and even check to see that there are funds. To actually modify the account though, the private key (issued at the time of a transaction) is needed.

Think of a Private Key as a one-way lock. An example is a library drop-off. You can put books inside, but you cannot remove them.

▸ SSL/TLS (Secure Socket Layer/Transport Layer Security) cryptographic protocols use both types of encryption. These protocols are used by many devices to provide security during communications over the Internet. The main steps to this protocol are:

  – Establishing a connection: one device attempts to connect to a second device

  – Handshake protocol: each party proves they are who they say they are using a public key and a private key.

      a. This step takes the longest. Like the credit card example, both parties need to prove that they are who they say they are.

      b. A Certificate Authority issues a digital certificate to verify that the encrypted key is owned by the site being contacted.

  – After the handshake protocol is successful, communication is encrypted with one key (symmetric encryption). If the handshake protocol is not successful, the entire SSL/TLS protocol must be reattempted.

  – Public Key Encryption is used during the handshake protocol of SSL/TLS.

  – Symmetric Encryption is used for the remainder of the time two parties are exchanging information after the handshake step is completed.

E. The Internet's open standards mean that it can be vulnerable to attacks.

1. Such attacks include: cyberwarfare or cybercrime.

2. Both of these involve stealing information in order to harm others. Examples include:

    i. Phishing: collecting information from others; people choosing to share private information may not realize it could be used to hurt them.

    ii. Viruses: software that uses system processing or memory from another person's computer to do harm to others or to that person.

    iii. Denial of Service (DOS) or Distributed Denial of Service Attacks (DDOS): flooding a part of the Internet with requests that are not real, so that the location is too busy dealing with false requests and can no longer handle real requests that need to be handled.

3. There are systems that can be used to prevent unauthorized access to private data.

    i. These systems include antivirus software and firewalls.

    ii. Like cybersecurity protocols, these devices are also constantly evolving.

SAMPLE MULTIPLE-CHOICE QUESTIONS RELATED TO THE INTERNET

A. Know the difference between the bandwidth and latency of a system.

EXAMPLE 1:

Suppose a bandwidth test of your Internet tells you that your download speed is 40 megabytes per second and that your upload speed is 6 megabytes per second. Which of the following are NOT possible explanations for this difference?

(A) The Internet Service Provider controls this so sites download as fast as possible for users.

(B) More information is downloaded per second than uploaded per second.

(C) A download has greater latency than an upload.

(D) An upload has less latency than a download.

Answer: (C)

A higher bandwidth means more data is passed. It also means less time passes for the same amount of data. Time passed is measured in latency. In general, uploads have less latency than downloads. (B) and (D) restate this. (A) explains why this difference is related to design.

B. Demonstrate that you understand the difference between examples of hierarchy and redundancy on the Internet.

EXAMPLE 2:

Which of the following are NOT caused by redundancy on the Internet? Select *two* answers.

(A) A link to a virus that can be downloaded accidentally from a site.

(B) The rerouting of a packet through a node due to a node being unavailable.

(C) The resending of a packet that was lost in processing.

(D) The mapping of a domain name to an IP address.

Answers: (A), (D)

Choice (A) is about a virus being accidentally downloaded by a person. This is not caused by the redundancy of the Internet; this is a person's mistake. Choice (D) is a mapping of a domain to an IP address. This supports making the Internet more accessible to people, but is not related to redundancy. Choices (B) and (C) specifically mention re-routing and re-sending, which are equivalent and are examples of redundancy.

Key Topics Related to Global Impact

I. OVERVIEW

A. You can expect about 10 percent of the multiple-choice questions on the End-of-Course Exam (7 out of 74 questions) to be about the topic of "Global Impact."

B. In addition, the Explore Performance Task has a writing prompt (Prompt 2c) that focuses on this topic (see Chapter 5).

II. WHAT IS GLOBAL IMPACT?

A. *Global impact* describes the impact that computing has had on the world.

B. These impacts include:

1. legal and ethical concerns

2. privacy and security concerns

3. the ability to connect in new ways with more people

4. the need for all people to understand computer science

III. WHAT YOU NEED TO KNOW AND UNDERSTAND ABOUT GLOBAL IMPACT

A. Computing has led to changes in the way people live around the world, including:

1. our society, economy, and culture

2. our ability to communicate, work together, and think about problems

3. our ability to solve new problems

B. Computing power increases have led to innovation.

1. Moore's Law predicted increases in computing power, specifically the rate of growth in an integrated circuit over time, which has encouraged industries to plan future research and development.

2. Advances in computing as a technology have generated and increased creativity and other fields.

C. The effects of computing are both beneficial and harmful.

1. Due to commercial access to music and movie downloads and streaming:

    i. laws have needed to change.

    ii. innovations have occurred to make it possible for people to do this legally.

2. Due to the amount of information available through digital means:

    i. laws related to controlling access to content and/or censoring have needed to change.

    ii. people have access to more information.

    iii. there is an ongoing debate between the rights of the individual to remain private and the rights of the society to use this information for its benefit.

D. Computing enhances the way we communicate and work together. Below is a list of computing functions that promote communication.

1. Email: These are messages sent from one IP address to another. Examples include: Gmail, Hotmail, Outlook, Yahoo.

2. SMS (Short Message Service): These are text messages to another person or group, commonly called "texting," usually supported by mobile phone services.

3. Chat rooms and chat messaging: These are websites, or parts of websites, where people select a "chat window" to communicate via text with groups or individuals. Visual chat rooms use virtual reality technology to add graphics to the chat environment. Examples include: Google Chat, Skype, Facebook Messenger, Second Life, IMVU.

4. Video conferencing and video chat: These occur in online environments called "chat rooms" where you can communicate with individuals or groups via video. Examples include: Skype, Google Hangouts, Facetime.

5. Social Media: These are websites or applications where you can share information and create communities. Examples include: Twitter, Facebook, LinkedIn, gaming communities such as World of Warcraft.

6. Cloud Computing: This is the ability of a business or individual to rent a network of servers on the Internet to store and process data, rather than use their own server or personal computer. Most major companies now offer cloud computing services. Examples include: Apple iCloud, Amazon Drive, Google Docs.

E. Computing provides widespread access to information. Here are a few examples:

1. Public data

   i. More data is available to the public now than ever before in our history as a society. This is largely due to the availability of online data. Examples include: census data, health data, government data, climate data.

   ii. People are generating new data via search trends and social media, which are often reassembled to produce new public data.

2. Search trends

    i.   Search results control where and what people see in response to their questions.

    ii.   People's searches indicate trends in a society or culture, and these searches are tracked and reported in social media, such as "trending" topics in Twitter.

3. Social media

    i.   The large number of online sharing websites have allowed people to spread more information faster than ever before. Examples include blogs, YouTube, Twitter, Facebook, LinkedIn.

F. Computing has changed how people interact with the physical world via emerging technology, including the following innovations:

    1. The Global Positioning System (GPS):

        i.   GPS relies on satellites, frequent updating from Earth's surface to cell phone towers, and other members of the network to be sure maps are accurate.

        ii.   Using GPS, you can navigate successfully in an unfamiliar location.

    2. Sensor networks:

        i.   These are networks of objects that collect data and report on the data collected.

        ii.   Using this innovation, for example, a self-driving car can tap into a sensor network of parking spaces in a large lot and find spaces that are not filled.

    3. Smart technologies:

        i.   A smart technology is one based on a sensor network, which when used with other members of a network, can solve a larger problem.

        ii.   Using this innovation, for example, a city could set up a Smart Parking solution to enable its parking slots with sensor networks to indicate when a space is free (or not). This Smart Transportation system would be able to suggest an area of the city most likely to have parking.

iii. Other examples include: smart grids, smart buildings, and smart transportation.

4. Technology that enhances human capabilities:

   i. Many innovations, such as wearable tech, enhance what human beings can do. People who consider these innovations to be a part of their identity often call themselves *cyborgs*.

   ii. Some of these innovations help you do something that you could not do without the technology. One common example is eyeglasses. This wearable technology enables you to see better than you would with just your natural vision. Innovative technology also helps people do things that human beings cannot normally do. For example, you could use artificial intelligence in vision enhancement to see things that you would not normally be able to see.

G. Computing has changed how people access daily activities such as shopping, health care, education, and entertainment. Here are a few examples:

1. E-commerce: People can purchase or sell products from their home using their computer.

2. Health care: People can contact their doctor using video conferencing, or research a health issue online to learn more about it.

3. Entertainment: Countless amounts of video, music, and images have been created and viewed by millions of individuals who otherwise may never have had the opportunity either to create or view these works.

4. Online learning: A person can view video, take courses, and work with others to learn, using video conferencing and other cooperative work environments. World-renowned

teachers post their approaches and lessons online for others to use.

H. Computing has helped people work together in a problem-solving process. Here are a few examples:

1. Citizen science: People collect and report data in a collective online location, such as a database. One example is *AgeGuess.org*.

2. Digitally-enabled collaboration: Digital tools are available to make online collaboration possible. Examples include video conferencing, public documents, or folders that can be shared in a common location on the Internet, blogs, and wikis.

3. Crowdsourcing: Digital environments can open up a project for people to provide their services and ideas. The idea is that the more people who work together to solve a problem, (1) the faster it will be solved, (2) the better the solution, and (3) the more will be learned. An example of this is called *github.com*.

I. Computing has caused innovation in many professional fields.

1. Machine learning and data mining

    i. This is the use of data and artificial intelligence to learn patterns in human behavior and make decisions based on these patterns.

    ii. Developments in these fields have led to innovation in medicine, business, and science.

2. Scientific computing

    i. This is the use of programming to compute quickly and to use computer models for making predictions.

    ii. Scientific computing has enabled innovation in science and business.

3. Information-sharing

   i.   People contribute works on information-sharing websites for others to use. Examples are Open Access, Creative Commons, and Wikimedia.

   ii.   Information-sharing promotes research via open and curated scientific databases.

IV. WHAT YOU NEED TO DO TO ANSWER QUESTIONS ABOUT GLOBAL IMPACT

A. Understand how computing has led to impacts.

EXAMPLE 1:

Which of the following is *not* an effect of the widespread access to digitized information?

(A) The Digital Millennium Copyright Act

(B) Accessing this information allows people to use or collect information about minors.

(C) Governments and/or law enforcement can access and track information about people that is shared publicly and use that information against them in legal cases.

(D) People no longer need a recording contract to sell their music; they can use this access to market to large audiences on social media and sell records independently.

Answer: (A)

This act was a control on this access. Options (B) through (D) are all effects.

Strategies for Success on the End-of-Course Exam

Your AP Computer Science Principles End-of-Course Exam will consist of 74 multiple-choice questions administered in one 2–hour testing session. The questions will be about Abstraction, Data and Information, Algorithms, Programming, the Internet, and Global Impact. A little more than 75 percent of this exam is about the first four topics. The Internet and Global Impact make up a little less than the remaining 25 percent of the exam.

The score you achieve on the multiple-choice section of the exam will be based on the number of questions you answer correctly. Each question has four options ((A) through (D)). The majority of the questions will have one correct answer. About eight of the 74 questions will have two correct answers, which are grouped together at the end of the exam. There is no partial credit, and there are no penalties for incorrect answers or unanswered questions.

You should have plenty of time to understand and answer each question, or at least to make an educated guess.

Here are some test-taking tips to keep in mind:

1. **Answer all related questions together.** One prompt may have more than one question related to that prompt. *Do not skip over these related questions.* Once you invest the time reading the prompt, skipping questions will mean you have to reread the prompt later, which will take away time from answering other questions.

2. **Use the process of elimination.** Success is as much about finding the correct answer as it is about getting rid of the wrong answers! Use your subject knowledge to cross out as many of the wrong answer choices as possible.

3. **Be ready to apply your skills and understanding.** The multiple-choice questions are not about vocabulary or recalling specific details of how a part of a computer or a computing innovation works. The questions are about applying what you know about these details to show your understanding and that you have practiced the necessary skills.

4. **Watch your time.** If you are spending more than 2 minutes on a question, make an educated guess and move on. If you finish your exam and you have time left, review your responses. If there are questions you have not answered, make your best guess.

5. **Answer all questions.** Points are not deducted for incorrect answers or unanswered question. It's in your best interest to answer all of the questions.

6. **Circle key command words in a question.** Circle such words as EXCEPT, ALL, NOT, or BEST. If you're reading the question quickly, you might miss seeing these all-important commands. Be sure to focus on the logic of the question.

7. **Pay attention to your bubble sheet.** Make sure that you have entered your answers correctly on the bubble sheet. If you're working on question 4, be sure you're filling in the bubble for question 4. If you lose your place and put the answer for question 4 in the bubble for question 5, it will throw off your entire answer sheet and thus your score!

8. **Think of your answer first.** Read the question and think of your answer first, before you read the answer choices given. This can help you select the best choice, rather than falling into distracting traps presented by wrong answer choices.

PART IV

APPENDICES

Glossary

abstract data types (ADT's)—lists and other collections used to develop programs

abstraction—to reduce detail or information for a purpose in a program; to help improve focus on a relevant concept; or to understand or solve a problem

algorithm—a step-by-step set of instructions implemented by a program to develop and express solutions to a computational problem

American Standard Code for Information Interchange (ASCII)—character encoding scheme used to translate characters into numerical values

anonymity software—software that hides your browsing history and prevents use of cookies to track your data

antivirus software—software that you install on your computer or network to prevent viruses from infecting your computer

append (in list operations)—adding an element to the end of a list

ASCII—*see* American Standard Code for Information Interchange

assignment—when you put a value into a memory location and give that location a name in a program; on the AP CS Principles exam, the assignment operator is represented with an arrow ($\leftarrow$)

authentication—a step in encryption that verifies that the recipient of the message is who should be receiving the message; *see* Certificate Authorities

bandwidth—*see* system bandwidth

binary search—a search algorithm that finds a target in an ordered set by halving the set being searched at each stage until the target is found or a set of one element is all that remains

binary number system—two-digit number system where each number represents a power of 2

bit—a single binary digit which can contain either a 1 or a 0

block-based language—one of two typical languages seen in the AP Computer Science Principles course; writing code in this language often involves dragging and dropping pictorial code, rather than typing text; *see* also text-based language

boolean logic—branch of algebra where all values are represented by either true or false

boolean data type—a variable that is either true or false

browser—*see* web browser

browsing history—list of web page addresses (and related data) that a person has viewed

capacity—*see* system capacity

central processing unit (CPU)—the part of a computer that manages processes

Certificate Authority (CA)—issues digital certificates that validate ownership of encrypted keys used in secured communications; used in authentication step of public key encryption; managed by public key infrastructure

circuit—a complete path that allows electrical current to flow from a high voltage to low voltage; fundamental concept used in component design to manipulate data (bits)

citizen science—collection and analysis of data by non-scientists on home computers; often performed in collaboration with professional scientists

client/server model (for network)—use of a central computer (server) to manage resources on a network

cloud computing/storage—rather than using a local computer, this form of computation uses a network of remote servers to calculate and/or store data; has fostered new ways to communicate and collaborate

clustering data—grouping data sets together to provide an argument that a pattern exists

complexity (of an algorithm)—the amount of logical reasoning (sometimes measured in lines of code) required to create an algorithm

computing—using computer algorithms to solve problems

condition—a decision in an algorithm based on a Boolean value (either true or false), used to control selection in an algorithm

constraint—limit placed to control inputs or outputs

cookie—information stored by a browser to track movement and information triggered by a person viewing a website

correctness (of a program)—depends on correctness of program components, including code segments and procedures

Creative Commons—a copyright license that can be used for free distribution while still ensuring proper attribution with appropriate citations

credibility—*see* source credibility

cryptography—the study of hiding messages or finding hidden messages

crowdsourcing—multiple people working (often online) together to complete a task

curated databases—database organized to facilitate research

cyberattack—attempt to penetrate, use, or access information on another computer or network without permission; examples include phishing or viruses

cybercrime—criminal activities carried out by using a computer or network

cybersecurity—technology, processes, and practices designed to protect digital data on networks and devices on these networks; includes hardware, software, and human components

cyberwarfare—use of technology by a nation-state, organization, or individual to disrupt or damage computers or networks of another nation-state or organization

database—a large collection of data that can be organized, searched, clustered, classified, transformed, displayed, and/or filtered to gain new insight or to make conclusions

data compression—technique that reduces the number of bits stored or transmitted; could be lossy or lossless

data mining—the analysis of large databases to retrieve new insights; example: artificial intelligence that has enabled innovation in medicine, business, and science

decidable problem—problem in which an algorithm can be constructed to answer "yes" or "no" for all inputs

desktop computer—personal computer meant to stay in one place

digital certificate—forms digital connection between the identity of the recipient and the public key on this certificate; used for authentication step of public key encryption; managed by Certificate Authorities (CAs)

"digital divide"—expression for the differing access to computing and the Internet based on socioeconomic or geographic characteristics of a population

distributed denial-of-service (DDoS) attacks—compromise performance of a device that is on a network by flooding it with requests from multiple systems

distributed system—model where multiple networked components communicate and coordinate their actions by passing messages to accomplish a task

domain name syntax—hierarchical definition of what a domain should look like; for example: rea.com. The "." character marks the location of the type of address this is. To the right of the "." is "com". This syntax will then look for where "rea" is located among all "com" addresses.

data streaming—transfer of data at a high rate from the sender to the receiver through a network. Example: used by music services and movie providers to provide content to users.

decryption—using mathematical algorithms to decode (decipher) a message; usually this algorithm is used to protect encrypted information from unauthorized viewers; *see* encryption

Digital Millennium Copyright Act (DMCA) of 1998—legislation passed to protect copyrighted digital data while also making it more widely available

domain name system (DNS)—a hierarchical naming system designed to identify individual entities on the Internet or any network; was not designed to be completely secure

domain name server—translates domain names to Internet Protocol (IP) addresses

efficiency (of an algorithm)—measure of the execution time and memory usage of an algorithm; often represented using Big-O notation

email—message from one computer to one or more recipients via a network; has fostered a new way to communicate and collaborate

element (of a list)—one specific item in a list

encryption—using mathematical algorithms to encode (hide) a message so only those that should read it can read it; *see* symmetric encryption and public key encryption

filtering data—removing parts of data sets to simplify data and/or to make conclusions more evident

firewall—part of a computer system or network that monitors incoming and outgoing communication and decides what will be allowed to travel (in or out) based on security rules

floating-point value—used in a programming language to represent non-integers

Global Positioning System (GPS)—network of orbiting satellites that are used by devices on earth to calculate the exact speed or location of the device on earth; example of a technology that has changed how humans travel, navigate, or find information related to geolocation

hardware component—physical part of a computer

heuristic—algorithmic approach applied to improve an algorithm that is based on finding solutions among all available options using a general set of rules; may result in approximate solutions instead of exact solutions; may be helpful to find solutions in reasonable time; may be helpful to find approximate solutions to unsolvable problems

hexadecimal number system—sixteen-digit number system where each number represents a power of 16

hierarchical system—system where devices and protocols are in an interdependent relationship and ordered into several levels; every member of this system has some other member above it and another member below it with the exception of the top level

hypertext transfer protocol (HTTP)—standard for how files are transferred on the Internet

hypothesis—a guess about how one action may cause another action to occur

index (of a list)—location in a list, must be a number greater than 0 or less than or equal to the length of the list in the end-of-course exam

input (to a procedure)—the data that an algorithm needs to be able to run

integrated circuit—one of the hardware components of a computer, sometimes called a chip or microchip; it is a set of electronic circuits such as transistors and resistors that work together to accomplish a goal

intellectual property—invention created and credited to a person or corporation

internet—a connection of devices connected to each other via hardware, including routers, servers, and other devices, each of which is given an IP Address and must follow protocols

Internet, the—the worldwide connection of devices to each other via hardware including routers, servers, and other devices, each of which is given an IP address and must follow protocols

Internet Engineering Task Force (IETF)—develops and oversees Internet standards and Internet protocols

Internet Protocol (IP)—the way devices communicate with each other

Internet Protocol (IP) addresses—locations given to devices

Internet standard—evolving "rules" that govern how a device can join and/or communicate on the Internet

iteration (in an algorithm)—a loop or repeated behavior in an algorithm; one of three different parts of any algorithm (*see* sequencing and selection)

key (in encryption or decryption)—variable applied to a block of text to encrypt or decrypt that text; the length of the key is a factor in the security and performance of encryption algorithms

latency—*see* system latency

linear search—a search algorithm that finds a target by looking at each item, one at a time, until the end of the set is reached or the target is found

list—a collection of data in which each item is identified by a corresponding index

logic gate—one of the building blocks of a computer chip, logic gates typically take two inputs and return either true or false; combinations of operations of gates can create different streams of logic used in calculations and processes in advanced chips such as integrated circuits

lossless data compression—data compression technique where the number of bits needed to store or transmit information is reduced and the original data can be completely reconstructed

lossy data compression—data compression technique where the number of bits needed to store or transmit information is reduced, but the original data cannot be reconstructed

machine learning—the ability of a computer to learn without being explicitly programmed; example: artificial intelligence that has enabled innovation in medicine, business, and science

memory—any physical device in a computer that stores information

metadata—data about data that provides additional information; this data can be descriptive data about an image, a web page, or other complex object

mobile computer—any personal computing device not constrained to a desktop

model—a way of representing a real situation in a more abstract way (with less detail)

modulus—mathematical operation that returns the remainder (for example, the modulus of 12 and 5 is 2)

Moore's Law—prediction that the number of transistors per square inch on an integrated circuit will double each year; has encouraged industries that use computers to plan future research and development based on increases in computing power

network—group of two or more systems linked together

open access—online research sources that are available for anyone to use

output (of an algorithm)—what is made available after the input data is transformed by an algorithm

overflow error—error caused when a number is too large for the memory allocated for it. For example, the decimal value of the non-integer ⅓ is a non-terminating decimal. There is no way for a computer to allocate an infinite number of bits so the computer stores this number using the highest number of bits possible. The user needs to know this and not assume that the value is exact.

packet—way in which data is packaged during data transfer on a network

parameter—input to a procedure

peer-to-peer network—network that does not follow the client/server model; members of this network are of equal value and share resources

phishing—cybercrime where a website, email, or other digital form of communication attempts to obtain personal information from a person by disguising itself as something that the person would normally use to share this information

plagiarism—occurs when one person presents another's ideas as their own

procedure—named grouping of programming instructions code used to manage complexity or repeated code in a program

process—a behavior that uses memory, a central processing unit, input, and output that can execute alone or at the same time as other processes

processor—the main controller (or "brain") of a computer; it decides which process(es) will run, for how long, and what inputs to provide and what outputs to receive and share with these processes; uses RAM and ROM to manage memory needs

program—set of computer instructions assembled to help us create, analyze, understand, and/or solve problems or to automate a process

programming language—computer instructions used to translate human ideas into software

proxy server—allows user to make connection to another network service without going through the local server that the person would normally need to use

pseudocode—words used to organize thoughts to help plan writing code; pseudocode helps programmers translate specifications (requirements) into code

public key encryption—asymmetric encryption scheme; involves two keys (one private and one public) where anyone can use the public key to encrypt a message, but only the sender and recipient know the private key so their data is protected

public key infrastructure—supports distribution and identification of public encryption keys so before information is exchanged the identity of the other party is verified (authenticated)

random access memory (RAM)—one of two memory types (*see* Read Only Memory) used by a computer processor; this memory is temporary, used to perform an action, and erased when the action is completed and when the computer is powered off

read only memory (ROM)—one of two memory types (*see* Random Access Memory) used by a computer processor; this memory is permanent and is available even after the computer is powered off

reasonable time—way to analyze an algorithm in terms of the number of steps required to solve a problem. An algorithm is said to run in reasonable time if the number of steps the algorithm takes is less than or equal to a polynomial function (constant, linear, square, cube, etc.) of the size of the set.

redundant system—system that is self-checking to improve system reliability

round-off error—caused with operations on floating-point values; an example is a computer trying to store $\frac{1}{3}$. A computer cannot store $\frac{1}{3}$ since it has infinitely repeating digits. Each machine would manage this differently based on the fixed number of bits allocated.

router—device that supports the connection between two or more networks

routing (of packets)—way in which data is sent on a network

scientific computing—use of advanced computing capabilities to understand and solve complex and often multidisciplinary problems; has enabled innovation in science and business

search engine—a website that allows you to search the Internet and uses algorithms to decide the best match to what you searched

secure sockets layer/transport layer security (SSL/TLS)—standards for sharing information and communicating between browsers and servers

segments (of a program)—smaller parts of a procedure; segments of code combine to create a procedure

selection (in an algorithm)—using a condition to control the logical path taken by an algorithm; one of three different parts of any algorithm (*see* selection, sequencing, and iteration)

semantic error—the code as written does not perform as planned when it runs; depends on your logic

sensor—device that detects, measures, records, or responds to a physical property

sequencing (in an algorithm)—ordering the steps of an algorithm; one of three different parts of any algorithm (*see* selection and iteration)

sequential search—*see* linear search

server—device that manages access and responds to requests on a network

short-circuit (in boolean logic)—when the result of a logical expression can be evaluated without seeing the entire expression; two examples:

(1) TRUE or _____ is always TRUE. It does not matter what comes after the "or."

(2) FALSE and _____ is always FALSE. It does not matter if what is in the blank is TRUE or FALSE.

short message service (SMS)—short text message, has fostered a new way to communicate and collaborate

simple mail transfer protocol (SMTP)—standard for how email messages are sent and received on the Internet

simulation—a program created to model a real situation with less detail to understand or solve a problem

size—*see* system size

smart technology—technology that responds to the user and/ or the environment; examples include smart grids, smart buildings, and smart transportation

social media—online applications that allow people to share information and connect with others; has fostered a new way to collaborate and communicate

solvable problem—a problem that can be solved exactly using an algorithm

source credibility—deciding if a source is reliable based on the reputation and credentials of the author(s), publisher(s), site owner(s), and/or sponsor(s)

specifications—the key details that need to be included in an algorithm; examples: elements defined in the specifications are the inputs, outputs, data types, and name(s) of procedures called or being created

symmetric encryption—method of encryption involving one key for encryption and decryption

syntax error—the written code does not match the computer language; often produces a compile error when you try to run your program

system bandwidth—measure of amount of data (measured in bits) that can be sent in a fixed amount of time

system capacity—amount of bits that could be stored on a system

system latency—time elapsed between the transmission of request and receipt of a reply; round trip time

system size—amount of bits that can be stored on a system

targeted advertising—form of advertising that uses data available about a consumer to appeal to that consumer directly

text-based language—one of two types of languages commonly seen in programming; usually created using a text editor that may or may not need to compile to run; *see* block-based language

transistor—one of the building blocks of a computer chip, controls flow of electricity by amplifying or redirecting it

undecidable problem—problem in which no algorithm can be constructed to answer "yes" or "no" for all inputs

unsolvable problem—a problem that cannot be solved exactly using any algorithm

virus—code that is capable of duplicating itself; often disrupts or damages data

web browser—program on computer that allows you to visit websites; this program runs on your computer when you type website addresses; the browser displays the files located at that address; browsers are governed by protocols set by the Internet Engineering Task Force, including hypertext transfer protocol and secure sockets layer/transport layer security.

World Wide Web—the set of interconnected documents identified by the hyperlinks and Uniform Resource Locators (URLs) or information space of the Internet.

Programming Languages and Resources to Learn Programming

Language	Website (for downloads and links to learn)	Brief Description	Type of Programming Language
Alice	alice.org	Allows you to create a story in a 3D environment	Both text and block
App Inventor	ai2.appinventor.mit.edu	Create apps for Android devices	Block-based language
App Lab	code.org/educate/applab	Code.org's environment to develop online apps	Block-based with transition to text
Java	There are several development environments for java. The most popular for standard development are: • Eclipse (eclipse.org) • Bluej (bluej.org)	Allows you to create text-based programs or to code in other environments that would require Java to begin (examples: Android Development Environment or Java with Greenfoot—greenfoot.org, using Java to make games)	Text
JavaScript	javascript.com	Used to create code that runs in an online browser	Text
Lego Mindstorms NXT	nxtprograms.com	For use with lego robots such as the EV3	Block
Pencil Code	pencilcode.net	Create art, music, and/or a story using code	Block or text
Processing	processing.org	Learn to code in context of visual arts	Text
Python	python.org	Readable language; allows you to code between systems on most computers	Text

(continued)

Language	Website (for downloads and links to learn)	Brief Description	Type of Programming Language
R	R-project.org and Rstudio.com	Language used in statistical analysis	Text
Scratch	scratch.mit.edu	Create characters and narrate their behavior with code	Block
Snap!	snap.berkeley.edu	Extension of Scratch; allows class creation	Block
Swift	developer.apple.com/swift	Write apps that will run on an apple device	Text

Converting Between Number Systems

I. COUNTING IN OUR NUMBER SYSTEM

Consider the decimal number 509 in our number system. You would say it as "five hundred nine." When you say it, you hear the *worth* of the 5 is much greater (5 *hundred*) than that of the 9. This "0" value is not spoken. The place value increases from right to left, and place value matters much more than the digits.

100	10	1
5	0	9

In our decimal number system we have 10 digits: 0, 1, 2, 3, 4, 5, 6, 7, 8, and 9. In any number system that we will discuss for this course, place value increases from right to left. Notice that each place value is a power of 10 higher than the place value to its right.

$$509 = 9*1 + 0*10 + 5*100$$
$$= 9*10^0 + 0*10^1 + 5*10^2$$

You might see the number 509 in terms of its place value, or the "bucket" each digit is placed in to tell you its worth.

To understand a different number system, we need to think about the word "digit." As humans, we have 10 digits (fingers) and we have been taught from a young age to count to 10 on these fingers: 1, 2, 3, 4, 5, 6, 7, 8, 9, 10. The problem with this is that the last number (10) involves *two* digits (0 and 1). Instead, our ten digits are 0, 1, 2, 3, 4, 5, 6, 7, 8, 9. In fact, all number systems will start with the number 0.

0
1
2
3
4
5
6
7
8
9
10
11
12
13
Counting in Decimal Number System

Let's look at what this means as we count in our decimal number system. Notice how when we run out of digits (we reach 9), a new digit is added to the left of the 9 and the place value that held the 9 is reset to 0. This would happen again at 19. 19 + 1 = 20. The place value that held the 9 becomes a 0 and the place value to the left of the 9 is increased by 1. The hundreds place needs to be introduced for the first time to handle 99 + 1. Since both the ones and the tens place are "filled" with the largest digit, the hundreds place is needed: 99 + 1 = 100.

II. COUNTING WITH DIFFERENT NUMBER SYSTEMS

Decimal	Binary	Hexadecimal
0	0	0
1	1	1
2	10	2
3	11	3
4	100	4
5	101	5
6	110	6
7	111	7
8	1000	8
9	1001	9
10	1010	A
11	1011	B
12	1100	C
13	1101	D
14	1110	E
15	1111	F
16	10000	10
17	10001	11
Comparing Counting in Number Systems		

A. Binary Number System:

Counting in the binary number system is very different from our number system. To start, there are two digits: 0 and 1. Think about how our decimal number system handled 9 (introduction of a new place value *and* resetting to 0).

Now, let's count a few numbers in binary:

0 – the first number (and digit) in any number system

1 – the second number in any number system

10 – we ran out of digits so we need a new place value

11 – increment place value on the right first

100 – ran out of digits so we need a new place value

With just these first five numbers, you can see:

1. binary numbers are helpful since this is how a machine (computer) understands information;

2. binary numbers require a lot more place values to express a value than we need in our number system.

B. Hexadecimal Number System

The hexadecimal number system has 16 (hex represents 6, decimal for 10) digits. Like any number system, it starts at 0. However, at 9 we run out of numerical digits. So we use letters to represent a single digit. The digit A represents 10, B represents 11, and so on until F represents 15.

Looking at hexadecimal digits next to decimal digits you might not notice the advantage of hexadecimal numbers right away. The major advantage is that each digit is worth more. Notice how to represent the decimal number 17 in hexadecimal all that you need is 11. Also notice how the decimal number 12 *requires* two digits in our number system but only one digit (C) in the hexadecimal number system.

C. Conversions

1. Decimal to Binary

To understand how to convert this value to a different number system, we have to think of numbers in terms of these types of buckets. The buckets we are used to understanding are powers of 10. Remember 509. See the image at right. $10^0 = 1$, $10^1 = 10$, and $10^2 = 100$.

100	10	1
5	0	9

Suppose we want to convert 509 to binary digits (or "bits"). We will need to think in powers of 2. $2^0 = 1$, $2^1 = 2$, $2^2 = 4$, $2^3 = 8$, and so on. 512 is a power of 2 that is too large for 509, so this will be an unnecessary place value. The next lowest is 256. $509 - 256 = 253$. We will need to find digits to hold a value of 253. The next digit is worth 128. Again, $253 - 128 = 125$.

This pattern continues until the total value of 509 is stored in binary digits.

256	128	64	32	16	8	4	2	0
1	1	1	1	1	1	1	0	1

Try this out on a separate piece of paper by following these steps:

(1) Write a table of place values (powers of 2).

 ▸ Place values increase from right to left

 ▸ The highest power of 2 is the highest number that can go into the value you are trying to convert without going over it.

(2) Fill in 1 or 0 from left to right.

 ▸ If the place value is used (number is a 1), subtract from the original value.

 ▸ Repeat until each position has a 1 or 0

(3) The number on the bottom of the table is a binary representation of the original value.

Based on the above, we know that 509 in decimal digits is equivalent to 111111101. We can convert back from binary digits to the decimal number system:

$$111111101 = 1(2^0) + 0(2^1) + 1(2^2) + 1(2^3) + 1(2^4) +$$
$$1(2^5) + 1(2^6) + 1(2^7) + 1(2^8)$$
$$= 1 + 0 + 4 + 8 + 16 + 32 + 64 + 128 + 256$$
$$= 509$$

2. Decimal to Hexadecimal

Suppose we want to convert 509 to hexadecimal digits.

▸ We will need to think in powers of 16. $16^0 = 1$, $16^1 = 16$, $16^2 = 256$, $16^3 = 4096$, and so on.

▸ Each place value can have a number as high as 15 (which will change to a letter if 10–15)

	100	10	1	
$509 =$	5	0	9	$= 1FD$

4096 is a power of 16 that is too large for 509, so this will be an unnecessary place value. The next lowest is 256. 509 – 256 = 253. We will need to find digits to hold a value of 253. The last two digits are more complicated. Using long division, 253/16 = 15 with a remainder of 13. In the hexadecimal number system, however, 15 is F. The remainder, 13, is written as D. So 509 in decimal is equivalent to 1FD. To convert back from the hexadecimal number system to the decimal number system:

$$1FD = D(16^0) + F(16^1) + 1(16^2) = 13(16^0) + 15(16^1)$$
$$+ 1(16^2)$$
$$= 13 + 240 + 256 = 509$$

3. Binary to Hexadecimal and Hexadecimal to Binary

Notice how every four binary digits is equal to one hexadecimal digit since $2^4 = 16$. We can use this to our advantage when converting between binary and hexadecimal number systems.

Looking at the same example, we know that
111111101 = 1FD.

If I spread these digits out, four bits at a time, starting from the right most position:
1 1111 1101 = 1 F D

Look at each four-bit cluster. 1101 is equal to 1 + 4 + 8 = 13. D is also equal to 13.

Similarly, 1111 = F. 1 is equal to 1. Four bits at a time, we can make direct conversions!

High-Level to Low-Level Abstractions

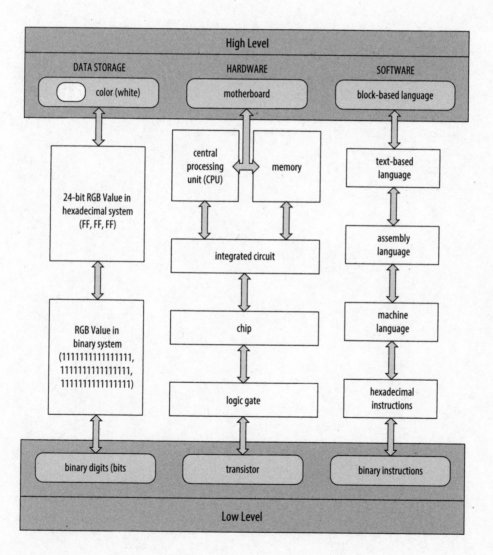

Explore Performance Task Checklist

This is a summary of the key requirements to maximize your score for the Explore Performance Task. It was created based on the June 2017 grading of this performance task.

Before using it, here are a few points to keep in mind:

- After the exam, your results for the Explore Performance Task will be given to you by "Reporting Category."

  - These categories are what graders will use to assign a score to your task.

  - To line up with this, the following checklist also uses that language and explains the connection to the Performance Task in the second column.

  - To make it easier for you to check your performance task, these requirements are organized by prompts.

- Remember that a computing innovation is an innovation that works because of a computer or a program code. The innovation may be:

  - physical but with computational processes being called to make decisions (like a self-driving car)

  - non-physical computer software (like a cell phone app)

  - a computing concept (like social networking, since it requires use of the Internet)

Before starting the checklist, write down your COMPUTING INNOVATION here:

Then use this checklist to be sure you did all you could to maximize your score for your Explore Performance Task.

Reporting Category	Performance Task Connection	What you need to do to maximize your score for each category:
Using Development Processes and Tools	Computational Artifact	☐ Your performance task is about a computing innovation (it works because of a computer and program). ☐ This computing innovation is identified clearly in the artifact ☐ You used a computer as a tool to create the computational artifact. ☐ Your artifact shows the purpose, function, and effect of this computing innovation.
Analyzing Impact of Computing, 1 of 2	Writing Prompt 2a	☐ Your response here is about your computing innovation. ☐ Your response states a fact about the computing innovation's purpose (why it was created) or function (how it works).
Analyzing Impact of Computing, 2 of 2	Writing Prompt 2c	☐ Your response is about your computing innovation. ☐ Your response identifies a beneficial effect of the computing innovation working as intended. ☐ Your response explains how the beneficial effect impacts society, economy, or culture. (To do this, you have written about a way in which your innovation benefits all people, whether or not they own or use the innovation.)

(continued)

Reporting Category	Performance Task Connection	What you need to do to maximize your score for each category:
Analyzing Impact of Computing, 2 of 2 *(con't)*	Writing Prompt 2c *(con't)*	☐ Your response argues how the beneficial effect is connected to more than one person. The argument clearly connects the innovation to the effect and explains why this effect is significant.
		☐ Your response is focused on a beneficial effect that happens as a result of the innovation working as it was intended.
		☐ Your response identifies a harmful effect of the computing innovation working as intended.
		☐ Your response explains how the harmful effect impacts society, economy, or culture. (To do this, you have written about a way in which your innovation harms all people, whether or not they own or use the innovation.)
		☐ Your response argues how the harmful effect is connected to more than one person and identifies a significant result of this effect. The argument clearly connects the innovation to the effect.
		☐ Your response is focused on a harmful effect that happens as a result of the innovation working as it was intended.

(continued)

Reporting Category	Performance Task Connection	What you need to do to maximize your score for each category:
Analyzing Data and Information	Writing Prompt 2d	☐ Your response here is about your computing innovation.
		☐ You identify data that is processed by the computer or program code that makes the computing innovation work.
		☐ You reduced the data to a type that shows a connection to the computer. The type might be a number (integer), Boolean, text, image, video, audio, or a signal.
		☐ You explain how the data is consumed, produced, or transformed by the key computer or program code that makes your computing innovation work.
		☐ You identify one data storage, privacy, or security concern and you explain how it is related to the data being processed by the computing innovation.
		☐ You explain the consequence of the concern.

(continued)

Reporting Category	Performance Task Connection	What you need to do to maximize your score for each category:
Finding and Evaluating Information	Writing Prompt 2e	☐ You checked the dates on your sources. At least two of the sources were created after the end of last school year.
		☐ For each online source, you included the permanent URL, identified the author, title, source, date retrieved and, if possible, the date posted.
		☐ For each print source you included the author, title of excerpt/article and magazine or book, page number(s), publisher, and date of publication.
		☐ If you used an interview source, you included the name of the person interviewed, the date of the interview, and the person's position in the field.
		☐ You used in-text citations to connect your paper to its source.
		☐ Your sources are relevant, credible, and easily accessed.

Create Performance Task Checklist

This is a summary of the key requirements to maximize your score for the Create Performance Task. It was created based on the June 2017 grading of this performance task.

Before using it, here are a few points to keep in mind:

- After the exam, your results for the Create Performance Task will be given to you by "Reporting Category."

  - These categories are what graders will use to assign a score to your task.

  - To line up with this, the following checklist also uses that language and explains the connection to the Performance Task in the second column.

  - To make it easier for you to check your performance task, requirements are organized by prompts.

- Remember that the program you created to accomplish this task is the "center" of your performance task. You (1) designed, (2) debugged, (3) tested, and (4) documented your program to do one of the following:

  - help solve a problem

  - enable an innovation

  - express a personal interest

Before starting the checklist, write down a name for your program here:

Next, write down the purpose of the program here:

| |
| |

Then use this checklist to be sure you did all you could to maximize your score for your Create Performance Task.

Reporting Category	Performance Task Connection	What you need to do to maximize your score for each category:
Developing a Program with a Purpose	Video & Response 2a	☐ The video shows at least one feature of the program running. ☐ The video is unbroken. ☐ The written response or the video identifies the program's purpose (what the program is attempting to do).
Developing a Program with a Purpose	Response 2b	☐ You described or outlined steps used in the incremental and iterative development process to create the entire program. ☐ You identified and explained two difficulties, two opportunities, or one difficulty and one opportunity ☐ You described how you resolved both, and how this resolution made your final program better ☐ Both are related to the program's purpose.

(continued)

Reporting Category	Performance Task Connection	What you need to do to maximize your score for each category:
Applying Algorithms	Code in Response 2c and Response 2c	☐ The code you selected shows an algorithm (has sequences of instructions that use sequencing, selection, or iteration)
		☐ You created the selected algorithm.
		☐ The selected algorithm uses mathematical concepts (expressions that use arithmetic operators and mathematical functions) or logical concepts (Boolean algebra or Boolean expressions)
		☐ The prompt explains how the selected algorithm functions
		☐ The prompt describes what the selected algorithm does to accomplish the overall purpose of the program.
		☐ The selected algorithm shows one algorithm that includes at least two or more algorithms.
		☐ At least one of the two included algorithms uses mathematical or logical concepts.
		☐ The written response explains how one of the included algorithms functions alone.

(continued)

Reporting Category	Performance Task Connection	What you need to do to maximize your score for each category:
Applying Abstraction	Code in Response 2d and Response 2d	☐ The code you selected shows an abstraction you created.
		☐ The written response explains how the selected abstraction manages the complexity of the program.
		☐ The written response explains how managing the complexity helped with accomplishing the purpose of this program.

Exam Reference Sheet

Instruction	Explanation
Assignment	
Text: a ← expression Block: ⟮ a ← expression ⟯	Evaluates expression and assigns the result to the variable a.
Text: DISPLAY(expression) Block: ⟮ DISPLAY expression ⟯	Displays the value of expression, followed by a space.
Text: INPUT () Block: INPUT	Accepts a value from the user and returns it.
Arithmetic Operators and Numeric Procedures	
Text and Block: a + b a − b a * b a / b	The arithmetic operators +, −, *, and / are used to perform arithmetic on a and b. For example, 3/2 evaluates to 1.5.
Text and Block: a MOD b	Evaluates to the remainder when a is divided by b. Assume that a and b are positive integers. For example, 17 MOD 5 evaluates to 2.

(continued)

Instruction	Explanation
Arithmetic Operators and Numeric Procedures (continued)	
Text: RANDOM a,b Block: RANDOM a,b	Evaluates to a random integer from a to b, including a and b. For example, RANDOM (1, 3) could evaluate to 1, 2, or 3.
Relational and Boolean Operators	
Text and Block: a = b a ≠ b a > b a < b a ≥ b a ≤ b	The relational operators =, ≠, >, <, ≥, and ≤ are used to test the relationship between two variables, expressions, or values. For example, a = b evaluates to true if a and b are equal; otherwise, it evaluates to false.
Text: NOT condition Block: NOT condition	Evaluates to true if condition is false; otherwise, evaluates to false.
Text: condition1 AND condition2 Block: condition1 AND condition2	Evaluates to true if both condition1 and condition2 are true; otherwise, evaluates to false.
Text: condition1 OR condition2 Block: condition1 OR condition2	Evaluates to true if condition1 is true or if condition2 is true or if both condition1 and condition2 are true; otherwise, evaluates to false.

(continued)

Instruction	Explanation
Selection	

Text:
 	
``
IF (condition)
{
    <block of statements>
}
``
Block:
 	
IF condition
 	
block of statements
	The code in `block of statements` is executed if the Boolean expression `condition` evaluates to true; no action is taken if `condition` evaluates to false.

Text:
 	
``
IF (condition)
{
    <first block of statements>
}
ELSE
{
    <second block of statements>
}
``
Block:
 	
IF condition
 	
first block of statements
 	
ELSE
 	
second block of statements
	The code in `first block of statements` is executed if the Boolean expression `condition` evaluates to true; otherwise, the code in `second block of statements` is executed.

(continued)

Instruction	Explanation
Iteration	

Text:
 	
`REPEAT n TIMES`
`{`
 	
   `<block of statements>`
 	
`}`
 	
Block:
 	
REPEAT n TIMES
  block of statements
	The code in `block of statements` is executed n times.

Text:
 	
`REPEAT UNTIL (condition)`
`{`
 	
   `<block of statements>`
 	
`}`
 	
Block:
 	
REPEAT UNTIL condition
  block of statements
	The code in `block of statements` is repeated until the Boolean expression condition evaluates to true.

List Operations	
For all list operations, if a list index is less than 1 or greater than the length of the list, an error message is produced and the program terminates.	

Text:
`list[i]`
Block:
`list i`
	Refers to the element of `list` at index i. The first element of `list` is at index 1.

(continued)

Instruction	Explanation
List Operations (continued)	

Text:
 	
`list[i] ← list[j]`
 	
Block:
 	
`list i ← list j`
	Assigns the value of `list[j]` to `list[i]`.

Text:
 	
`list ← [value1, value2, value3]`
 	
Block:
 	
`list ← value1, value2, value3`
	Assigns value1, value2, and value3 to `list[1]`, `list[2]`, and `list[3]`, respectively.

Text:
 	
`FOR EACH item IN list`
`{`
 	
　`<block of statements>`
 	
`}`
 	
Block:
 	
`FOR EACH item IN list`
 	
　`block of statements`
	The variable `item` is assigned the value of each element of `list` sequentially, in order from the first element to the last element. The code in `block of statements` is executed once for each assignment of `item`.

Text:
 	
`INSERT (list, i, value)`
 	
Block:
 	
`INSERT list, i, value`
	Any values in `list` at indices greater than or equal to `i` are shifted to the right. The length of list is increased by 1, and `value` is placed at index `i` in `list`.

Text:
 	
`APPEND (list, value)`
 	
Block:
 	
`APPEND list, value`
	The length of `list` is increased by 1, and `value` is placed at the end of `list`.

(continued)

Instruction	Explanation
List Operations (continued)	
Text: REMOVE (list, i) Block: REMOVE list, i	Removes the item at index i in list and shifts to the left any values at indices greater than i. The length of list is decreased by 1.
Text: LENGTH (list) Block: LENGTH list	Evaluates to the number of elements in list.
Procedures	

Text:
 	
PROCEDURE name (parameter1,
              parameter2,...)
{
   <instructions>
}
Block:
 	
PROCEDURE name parameter1,
                 parameter2, ...
 	
   instructions
	A procedure, name, takes zero or more parameters. The procedure contains programming instructions.

(continued)

Instruction	Explanation
Procedures (continued)	

Text:
 	
`PROCEDURE name (parameter1,`
`            parameter2,...)`
`{`
 	
`    <instructions>`
 	
`    RETURN (expression)`
 	
`}`
 	
Block:
 	
	A procedure, name, takes zero or more parameters. The procedure contains programming instructions and returns the value of expression. The RETURN statement may appear at any point inside the procedure and causes an immediate return from the procedure back to the calling program.

Robot	
If the robot attempts to move to a square that is not open or is beyond the edge of the grid, the robot will stay in its current location and the program will terminate.	
Text: `MOVE_FORWARD ()` Block: 	The robot moves one square forward in the direction it is facing.
Text: `ROTATE_LEFT ()` Block: 	The robot rotates in place 90 degrees counterclockwise (i.e., makes an in-place left turn).

(continued)

Instruction	Explanation
Robot (continued)	
Text: ROTATE_RIGHT () Block: (ROTATE_RIGHT)	The robot rotates in place 90 degrees clockwise (i.e., makes an in-place right turn).
Text: CAN_MOVE (direction) Block: CAN_MOVE [direction]	Evaluates to true if there is an open square one square in the direction relative to where the robot is facing; otherwise evaluates to false. The value of direction can be left, right, forward, or backward.

Notes

Notes

Notes

Notes

Notes

Notes

Notes

Notes